True Crime Stories

48 Terrifying True Crime Murder Cases

List of Twelve Collection 1

Ryan Becker, True Crime Seven

TRUE CRIME Z

Copyright © 2020 by Sea Vision Publishing, LLC

All Rights Reserved.

No part of this publication may be reproduced, distributed, or transmitted in any form or by any means, including photocopying, recording, electronic or mechanical methods, without the prior written permission of the publisher, except in the case of brief quotations embodied in critical reviews and certain other non-commercial uses permitted by copyright law.

Much research, from a variety of sources, has gone into the compilation of this material. We strive to keep the information up-to-date to the best knowledge of the author and publisher; the materials contained herein is factually correct. Neither the publisher nor author will be held responsible for any inaccuracies.

ISBN: 978-1095117408

Table of Contents

Table of Contents *5*

List of Twelve Volume 1 .... *25*

Introduction *27*

1: Marjorie Orbin *31*

    A Grisly Find 32

    The Stripper and the Salesman 33

    Jay's Disappearance 34

    Suspicion is Raised 35

II: Christy Sheats *39*

    Fatal Meeting 40

    Downward Spiral 41

    Mixed Messages 43

    The Last Argument 45

III: Luka Magnotta *47*

The Early Years 47

Starving for Attention 49

Reaching the Tipping Point 51

The Investigation 52

On Trial 54

IV: Shari Tobyne 56

The Disbursement of Body Parts 56

A Family's Concern 57

Eliminating Hubby 58

Charges and Prosecution 60

V: David Michael Barnett 62

Deadly Sunday 63

Surrender 65

VI: Arunya Rouch 67

Going Back to The Beginning 68

Grocery Store Shooting 68

  Motives and Sentencing 69

VII: Brian Nichols..*72*

  Background 73

  Holding on to the Past..73

  Assault on The Justice System...74

VIII: Valerie Pape..*80*

  Getting Her Story Straight...81

  Political Friends..82

  The Sentencing...84

IX: Robert Bever..*85*

  Massacre on Magnolia Court 86

  Family Secrets...87

  Sentencing..89

X: Amy Bishop..*91*

  Background 92

  Tragic Meeting...94

XI: Bryan Uyesugi 96

Life-Changing Events 97

Job Stress 97

Background 98

Psychological History 99

The Day of the Shooting 100

The Capture 101

Trial, Sentencing, and Lawsuits 102

XII: Antoinette Renee Frank 105

A Department in Crisis 105

Pouring Gas on the Fire 107

A Betrayal of Trust 108

Interrogation and Trial 112

Noteworthy Discoveries 113

Conclusion 116

List of Twelve Volume 2 119

Introduction *121*

I: Blaine Norris and Ryan Trimble *123*

    The Opening Scene 124

    The Proposal and Rehearsal 125

    Lights, Camera, Action, and Murder 126

II: James Holmes *129*

    The Descent from Honor Roll to Darkness 130

    The Dark Knight and the Gunman 131

    The Aftermath 133

III: Elliot Rodger *134*

    Wanting to Belong 134

    Online Confessions and Declarations 136

    Carrying Out the Plan 141

IV: Zachery Bowen *146*

    War and Coming Home 147

    The Storm Within 148

How Do You Like Your Meat Cooked?...............................149

Self-Inflicted Justice 150

V: Byron Smith *152*

Setting the Trap 152

Justifying on Tape 155

VI: David A. Burke *156*

Out of Control 157

The Firing 157

A Tragic Mistake 158

The Deadly Skies...159

VII: George Hennard *161*

Anger at Sea..161

An Explosive Mix 162

The Luby's Massacre 163

VIII: James Edward Pough *167*

Mother's Little Helper 167

    Violent Behavior 168

    Reprocessed 169

    The Shooting Spree 171

    Pay Back at the Loan Office 172

IX: Howard Unruh 174

    Coming Home 175

    Paranoia in the Neighborhood 176

    Walk of Death 178

    Criminally Insane 181

X: Angela Simpson 183

    To Kill a Snitch 184

    Investigation and Conviction 186

    No Regrets 187

XI: Thomas Michael Lane 189

    A Broken Home 190

    Problems at School 190

  Cafeteria Massacre 191

  Charges, Competency, and Sentencing 193

XII: James Huberty.. *195*

  Background 196

  The Survivalist 197

  Life in San Ysidro 198

  Judgment Day 199

  After the Nightmare 203

Conclusion..*205*

List of Twelve Volume 3 ....*207*

Introduction *209*

I: Austin Harrouff *213*

  Frat Boy Behaves Strangely 214

  The Demon Made Him Do It 215

  A Grisly Feast 218

  The Dr. Phil Interview 219

    Self-Identity Investigation 220

II: Stanley Dean Baker *222*

    Hitchhiking Across America 223

    Carnage At The National Park 225

    Connecting The Dots 227

    Pride In Murder 229

III: Albert Fentress *232*

    The Eccentric Teacher 233

    Best Laid Plans Taken To The Extreme 235

    Releasing A Killer? 237

IV: Omaima Aree Nelson *240*

    Seeking A Better Life 241

    A Relationship Gone Bad 241

    Dressed To Kill 242

    An Excuse To Kill? 244

V: Antron Singleton *246*

Big Dreams...247

The Devil's Drug..248

Unusual Representation 251

VI: Mark Sappington *252*

What's A Mother To Do?..253

Hanging With The Wrong Crowd....................................253

Voices In His Head 255

Got To Get Away...258

VII: Alex Kinyua *260*

Major Crazy at Morgan..261

The Roommate 265

Father Turns In Son..266

VIII: Otty Sanchez *267*

Starting Early 268

Rocky Times 268

A Critical Moment..269

    Communication Breakdown 270

    By 5:00 a.m. 272

IX: Tyree Lincoln Smith *274*

    Spiraling Downward 275

    Do Not Disturb! 277

X: Joseph Oberhansley *280*

    Family Darkness 281

    Extreme Violence 282

    She Stood by Her Man 285

    Rejection Kills 286

XI: Gregory Scott Hale *288*

    No Answer 289

    My Hero 289

    Deadly Encounter 290

    Caught Just In Time? 293

XII: Joe Metheny *295*

Conclusion *304*

List of Twelve Volume 4 .... *307*

Introduction *309*

I: Jiverly Antares Wong *313*

    Resistant to Change 314

    Of Pride, Secrecy, and Conspiracies 314

    The Bottom Drops Out 316

II: Priscilla Ford *319*

    A Teacher's Descent into Darkness 320

    The Thanksgiving Massacre 322

    Sentencing 324

III: Adam Lanza *325*

    Challenge from Birth 326

    Lanza's Downward Spiral 327

    The Sandy Hook Shooting 328

IV: Brenda Spencer *331*

    No Place for A Child 332

    The Sin of The Father 333

    Comments from Behind the Barricade 335

    Sentencing 335

V: Jared Lee Loughner *337*

    From Coltrane to Chaos 339

    The Merchant of Fear 342

    The Unanswered Question 343

    Sentencing 345

VI: Seung Hui Cho *347*

    Sullen and Silent 348

    Jelly and Other Madness 348

    Pushed Too Far 349

VII: Charles Joseph Whitman *352*

    From Altar Boy to Madness 353

    The Tower 356

VIII: Mark Barton *360*

    Moving on Up 361

    True Colors 362

    An Investment into Terror 365

IX: Jennifer San Marco *368*

    Singing Her Way into Madness 369

    Pay Back 372

X: Michael Kenneth McLendon *373*

    Living on A Dead-End Street 374

    Deadly Family Matters 376

    The Chase 377

XI: Christopher Harper-Mercer *379*

    Mother and Son 380

    Strange Interests 381

    Breaking Point 382

XII: Dana Ewell *384*

Self-Absorbed 385

Backfire 386

The Plan 387

The Hit 389

The Investigation 392

Sentencing 396

Conclusion 397

About True Crime Seven 421

Explore the Stories of
The Murderous Minds

A Note

From True Crime Seven

Hi there!

Thank you so much for picking up our book! Before you continue your exploration into the dark world of killers, we wanted to take a quick moment to explain the purpose of our books.

Our goal is to simply explore and tell the stories of various killers in the world: from unknown murderers to infamous serial killers. Our books are designed to be short and inclusive; we want to tell a good scary true story that anyone can enjoy regardless of their reading level.

That is why you won't see too many fancy words or complicated sentence structures in our books. Also, to prevent the typical cut and dry style of true crime books, we try to keep the narrative easy to follow while incorporating fiction style storytelling. As to information, we often find ourselves with too little or too much. So, in terms of research material and content, we always try to include what further helps the story of the killer.

Lastly, we want to acknowledge that, much like history, true crime is a subject that can often be interpreted differently. Depending on the topic and your upbringing, you might agree or disagree with how we present a story. We understand disagreements are inevitable. That is why we added this note so hopefully, it can help you better understand our position and goal.

Now without further ado, let the exploration to the dark begin!

List of Twelve Volume 1

12 Terrifying True Crime Murder Cases

Introduction

WHY IS IT THAT WE ARE FASCINATED BY STORIES and news coverage about murders? What is it about a killers' morbid deeds that attract our interest? Some murders have become a permanent fixture in our popular culture. Books, movies, and even music have used particular murders as their subject matter. Perhaps our fascination with murderers arises as a vestige from our childhood. Perhaps we graduate from our childhood fascination with monsters to an adult fascination with murderers. Perhaps it is because murderers put into practice what we have all felt at times but could never conceive doing. After all, how many of us, in our most emotional moments, have felt like killing someone?

Between news coverage and popular culture, we have, intentionally or not, adopted beliefs about murders, many of which are inaccurate. Many of our assumptions about murders could lead us to a false sense of security. We may wrongly believe there is a certain profile or set of qualities that murderers possess, that will help us intuitively tell whether or not the person next to us could take a human life.

Interviews with murderers have led to some surprising discoveries:

1. Most murderers are not cold-blooded monsters that lack any sense of humanity. Most murderers are people who are suffering emotionally and have never received help.
2. Murderers do not kill indiscriminately or without reason. Murderers kill due to their distorted thinking.
3. Murderers are not born to kill; they almost have always experienced or witnessed extreme trauma when young. Examples being physical abuse, sexual abuse, domestic violence, and drug abuse. The Adverse Childhood Experience Scale assesses a person's exposure to ten different traumatic events. Most of us would meet one of these criteria. Interviews with murderers have shown that most of them have experienced between nine and ten of these events.

In this book, you will read about twelve murderers. These individuals were selected because they are unfamiliar to many of us. While they may be less well-known than those murderers who have been highly publicized, their crimes are no less heinous. The murderers who will be covered in this book include:

- Marjorie Orbin, a former stripper who killed and dismembered her husband. To date, only his torso has been found.
- Christy Sheats, a mother who shot her two daughters at the dinner table to spite her husband.
- Luka Magnotta, a former male stripper and porn star who videotaped himself stabbing a man to death with an ice pick and then mailed his body parts to political offices and schools.
- Shari Tobyne, who dismembered her husband and distributed his body parts across three different counties.
- David Michael Barnett, the 20-year-old who stabbed both of his grandparents to death.
- Arunya Rouch, a petite woman who shot up the grocery store where she worked and murdered one of her co-workers.

- Brian Nichols, who went on a killing spree in a Georgia courtroom and was convicted on 50 charges.
- Valerie Pape, a wealthy Scottsdale Salon owner, who dismembered her husband. The media dubbed her case the "Trunk Murders."
- Robert Beaver, the 18-year-old who, with his brother, murdered their entire family.
- Amy Bishop, a university professor who shot her coworkers because she did not receive tenure.
- Bryan Uyesugi, a Xerox repairman who shot eight of his co-workers, killing seven of them.
- Antoinette Renee Frank, a police officer who, while on duty, committed three murders and armed robbery.

I
Marjorie Orbin

"WHAT THIS SEEMS TO BE IS A REVELATION OF your very darkest side, ma'am," said Judge Arthur Anderson, as he stared at Marjorie Orbin during her sentencing hearing. "When that dark side is unleashed, it's about as dark as it gets," he continued.

The judge spoke these words from his bench on September 8th, 2004, in a courtroom in Phoenix, Arizona. It was the start of fall in Arizona, a welcome reprieve from the blistering heat of the summer. It was not only the torrid heat that ended however, but a dark chapter of this desert community's crime annals.

A Grisly Find

The residents of Phoenix enjoy a patchwork of preserved desert areas throughout the city. However, on October 23rd, 2004, the rugged beauty of the area was eclipsed by a morbid find at the corner of Tatum and Dynamite Road, in North Phoenix. The Phoenix Police Department's 911 call center received a panicked call from an individual who was hiking in the area.

Police quickly arrived at the desert location, and the hiker led them to a spot that was not far off from the residential streets that surrounded the reservation. When the officers reached the site, they instantly knew that this was not a routine call. Detective Dave Barnes, of the Missing Persons Unit, arrived on the scene minutes later. A putrid smell filled the air as Barnes walked toward a 50-gallon Rubbermaid bin. "As we walked up you could smell the death in the air. Once you smell it, you know what it is for the rest of your life...it's the first time I had ever seen anything like that, where it's – just a piece of body," he would later say.

Barnes removed the lid and carefully opened the black trash bag contained within. Inside the trash bag was the bloody, dismembered torso of an adult male. Barnes would later tell a reporter, "All of the insides, all of the internal organs, intestines were missing...I thought, 'Who could do this to a human being? Cut off his arms, his legs, his head?'"

The grisly find was located less than two miles from the home of Marjorie Orbin, who lived in the 17000 Block of North 55th Street. Butcher had a strong suspicion that he had just found the torso of her missing husband; Marjorie had filed a missing person's report on September 22nd, 2004.

Jay Orbin was the successful owner of Jayhawk International, a dealership that specialized in Native American Art. He frequently traveled for business purposes, and it was not unusual for him to be gone three weeks out of the month. It was through his business travels that Jay met Marjorie.

The Stripper and the Salesman

Marjorie had been married seven times before meeting Jay at the age of 35. Marjorie was unable to conceive children and had lived a life with herself as the central focus. She entered each relationship looking for her Prince Charming, but it never happened.

Michael J. Peter was a very successful businessman who had made millions creating upscale strip clubs around the world. Marjorie left Peter because she believed he was cheating on her.

She moved to Las Vegas, where she danced at a strip club. It was at this strip club in 1993 that she met Jay, who was traveling through Las Vegas. They had been dating for a while when Jay proposed to Marjorie, offering to pay for fertility treatments if she married him. Marjorie accepted Jay's proposal, and they got married at the Little White Wedding Chapel in Las Vegas.

Soon afterward, they moved to Phoenix, where Jay lived. Marjorie was able to conceive and gave birth to their son, Noah. The couple divorced in 1997 but continued to live together. Marjorie had problems with the IRS and did not want Jay's assets to be vulnerable.

Jay's Disappearance

September 8th, 2004, Jay was driving back to Phoenix from a business meeting when he got a call from his mother, wishing him a happy birthday. That call was the last time anyone spoke to Jay.

When Jay's parents, brothers, and friends called his home, Marjorie told them that he had gone on a business trip and would not be returning until September 20th. During that time, those who cared about Jay could not reach him on his cell phone. His parents and friends expressed their concern to Marjorie; however, she said she did not know what was going on with him.

People who spoke to Marjorie about Jay stated that she expressed little concern for his welfare. Jay's intended return date passed, and still, nobody could reach him. When they inquired with Marjorie, she continued to remain aloof to their concerns. After continued pressure from friends and family, a missing person's report was filed on September 22nd.

Suspicion is Raised

The Police Department assigned Detective Jan Butcher to the case. She interviewed Marjorie, who indicated that the last time she'd seen Jay was on August 28th, when he had attended his son's birthday. Butcher became suspicious of Marjorie on September 28th, after leaving voicemail messages for her before she called back. "I asked her to provide me the license plate of the vehicle Jay was driving. She said she would call me back. She never did. So, that was a little bit odd," she later told a reporter.

From that point on, Butcher's suspicions only continued to grow. Credit card and phone tower records indicated that Jay had arrived at his home in Phoenix on September 28th, which didn't match Marjorie's claim that she had last seen him on August 28th.

When detectives checked Jay's credit card records, they found that Marjorie was spending thousands of dollars, including purchasing a $12,000 baby grand piano, while the business account had a withdrawal of $45,000. Within one day of reporting Jay missing, she had liquidated a total of $100,000 from Jay's personal and business accounts.

A final cause for suspicion arose during a call that Detective Butcher made to Marjorie requesting that she take a polygraph test. Butcher heard Marjorie remark to someone in the background, "You know what? She wants me to take a polygraph tomorrow." A male voice replied, "You tell her to go f--- herself."

Butcher obtained a search warrant and went to Marjorie's home, accompanied by a SWAT team. The SWAT team forced their way in and encountered an adult male, Larry Weisberg. Larry was Marjorie's new boyfriend and the voice that had been heard in the background of the phone call. Weisberg was combative, resulting in police tasing him.

Police searched the premises and found a large number of credit cards belonging to Jay, plus his business checkbook, items that he always kept with him when traveling. Though police did not make any arrests, their surveillance of Marjorie deepened. It was shortly after Marjorie's home was searched that police found Jay's torso in the Rubbermaid bin in the desert.

DNA evidence confirmed the torso belonged to Jay Orbin. The Maricopa County Medical Examiner's Office inspected the torso and concluded Jay had been shot and his body frozen. At some point, the body had been defrosted, and a jigsaw was used to dismember and decapitate it.

When searching Jay's business, police found a packet of jigsaw blades, with some of the blades missing. The Medical Examiner's Office determined the blades from the business matched the cut marks on the torso, where the limbs and vertebrae were severed.

Detectives traced the UPC code on the Rubbermaid bin back to a Lowes Home Improvement store in Scottsdale. The detectives scored big when they viewed video from the store's surveillance cameras and saw Marjorie purchasing the Rubbermaid bin, trash bags, and black tape. Police detained Marjorie when they caught her forging Jay's signature while making a purchase at a Circuit City store.

Jay's remaining body parts were never found, nor the gun that was used to shoot Jay.

Marjorie and her boyfriend, Larry Weisberg, were arrested on December 6, 2004. Weisberg was offered immunity if he agreed to testify against Marjorie, who was sentenced to life in prison on October 1st, 2009.

II

Christy Sheats

Located just northeast of Houston, the City of Katy has a population of 16,158, according to 2015 statistics.

On June 24th, 2016, a 911 dispatcher received a chilling call. At first, the dispatcher did not hear a single voice talking to her, as was the norm for most calls. Rather, she could hear several voices in the background. Then she heard the sound of a female crying and the words, "Please. Forgive me. Please. Don't shoot." This was followed by a male voice that begged, "Please. Don't point that gun at her."

A gunshot sounded and the female voice yelled to the dispatcher, "I'm shot." The dispatcher answered, "Hello? What's the address?" There was no response. The phone went dead.

Fatal Meeting

That phone call originated from the home of Jason and Christy Sheats. Christy, age 42, born in Decatur, Alabama, as was Jason. They were childhood sweethearts, who eventually moved to Katy, Texas, raising their two daughters; 17-year-old Madison and 22-year-old Taylor.

Jason worked for Oxy, a Houston-based oil company, as an IT consultant. In recent years, the Sheats had experienced marital problems, and Jason was planning to divorce Christy. On the day of that fateful phone call, it was Jason's 45th birthday, and Christy had called a family meeting around 5:00 p.m. Jason and their daughters expected the meeting to be about the looming divorce.

The family gathered around the dining table. Within seconds, the unimaginable occurred. Christy pulled out a .38-caliber revolver that she had been hiding under the table. She pointed it at Taylor and shot her in the back as she tried to run away from the table. Christy then turned to Madison and shot her in the neck. Jason ran and took refuge behind the living room couch, before fleeing with his daughters out the front door.

The daughters only made it to the street before both of them collapsed. Christy started running toward Taylor, who was lying on the street, while a neighbor offered Jason shelter in her home. The police, who arrived in time to witness this chaos, used trees and parked cars as shields. They saw Christy kneeling over Taylor's body, ready to shoot her a second time. Police ordered her to drop the gun. When she refused, they shot her.

A medical helicopter took Taylor to a local hospital where she died on arrival. Madison and Christy's lifeless bodies lay on the street in front of their home. The gun that Christy used was a gift from her grandfather, to whom she was extremely close.

Downward Spiral

Christy was deeply impacted when her grandfather died in 2012. Compounding her grief was the fact that her grandmother died two months later. Jason would later tell detectives that his wife suffered from depression during this time and became a heavy drinker. She had been admitted to a private mental health hospital for suicide attempts three times over a four-year period. Jason stated that Christy took a variety of prescription medications and was seeing a therapist. A neighbor informed the police the couple had separated but then recently reconciled. Before the shooting, Christy had no history of violence toward others.

Christy had stopped working after the death of her grandfather. Previously, she had worked as a hairstylist, as an executive assistant to the vice-president of a transportation company, and as a receptionist at Clean Canvas Tattoo Removal. This was a part-time position that she had held from January 2015 to May 2015, when she was fired. The owner, John Hollis, had originally thought that Christy was the perfect fit for the job. In an interview with People, he stated, "She was very pleasant when she wanted to be. That was in front of customers." He went on, "The times when she wasn't pleasant were times were when I assumed that whatever was going on at home was getting to her."

Hollis also indicated that Christy had spent some time living in an apartment away from the rest of the family. She would flip flop in her explanations about this to Hollis, sometimes saying that she was separated from her husband and other times stating that she was going to divorce him. "It was erratic; it was highs-and-lows," Hollis continued. "I wouldn't say it was deterioration; I would say it was peaks and valleys."

Mixed Messages

The interviews conducted by the media with those who knew her and through the Sheats's active use of social media provide a different perspective on Christy. A friend, Catherine Knowles, commented to People Magazine, "She loves her daughters. I have no idea what could possibly make a mother who loves her daughters as much as she did – what could cause a person to snap? The part of Christy that I knew was a very kind, loving mother." Knowles continued, "Within 20 seconds of meeting her, we were talking about her being a mom. That was her mission in life, that was her everything – her two daughters."

On Daughter's Day in September of the year prior to the shooting, Christy posted the following message to her Facebook account:

"Happy Daughter's Day to my two amazing, sweet, kind, beautiful, intelligent girls," she wrote. "I love and treasure you both more than you could ever possibly know."

Three years before the shooting, Taylor posted the following message to her Facebook account, honoring her mother on Mother's Day:

"Mom, you are so selfless, as you always put our whole family before yourself and never ask for anything in return," the post read. "You're so kind and loving, as you always remind us of just how much you care and how proud you are of everything we do. You're so intelligent and fun to be around because I feel like I can talk to you for forever now about anything."

The post concluded: "You're one of the strongest people I know, if not the strongest, and you have had to overcome so much in your life, but you still manage to love us and put your everything into being a mom. You're so encouraging, as you always push us to do our absolute best, even when we can't muster up the strength to do it ourselves. You're such a blessing to have as a mother and friend, and I truly appreciate you and all that you do. Happy Mother's Day to my amazing mommy and I love you."

Two years before the shooting, Christy posted on her Facebook page: "I am truly a Southern gal. I was born in Alabama but have been living here in Texas for 15 years. I have two amazing daughters I simply adore… They are my everything! I thank God for every breath he allows me to take!!"

When a reporter for the Houston Chronicle interviewed one of Christy's neighbors, Austin Enke, he stated, "They were always cheerful and never depressed. You never heard anything bad about them." While another neighbor told a local news station, "The mother was nice. You wouldn't expect it if they told you this is what was going to happen. I don't think anybody, at least a sane person, would do that."

In one Facebook post, Christy referred to herself as being Baptist, as well as a conservative and strong supporter of the second amendment, which provides the right for gun ownership. In one Facebook post, she wrote, "It would be horribly tragic if my ability to protect myself or my family were to be taken away, but that's exactly what Democrats are determined to do by banning semi-automatic handguns."

The Last Argument

On the day of the killing, Christy and Jason had gotten into an argument over Taylor, who had a fiancée, Juan Sebastian Lugo. Taylor and Lugo started seeing each other in 2011, and he had given her a promise ring in 2013.

Christy wanted to ground Taylor and prohibit her from seeing Lugo. Jason argued that he was agreeable to grounding Taylor, but they could not forbid her from seeing Lugo. Others knew Jason to be a doting father to his daughters. The reason for Taylor's punishment was not known, but later that morning, Jason told Christy, "This would be the last birthday that you are going to ruin."

After the shooting, Madison Davey, a friend of the Sheats family, spoke to a local news reporter and related a conversation that he'd had with Jason on the morning of the shooting. According to Davey, Jason said he had told Christy on the day of the shooting, "Just shoot yourself. Make it easy on all of us, just shoot yourself." He said Christy replied back to him, "No, that's not what this is about, this is about punishing you.'" Davey then told the reporter, "I always knew something would happen, but I never thought she would do this. Christy was toxic for the family. She was mentally unstable…He [Jason] would do anything to protect them and he tried to, but Christy was out to kill that day."

Police believe that Christy shot their daughters because that would cause the greatest pain for Jason, adding that Christy could have easily just killed Jason if she wanted. Knowing how much Jason loved his girls, killing them, and letting him live would create the greatest suffering for him.

III

Luka Magnotta

LUKA MAGNOTTA, WHOSE BIRTH NAME WAS ERIC Clinton Kirk Newman, was born July 24th, 1982, in Scarborough, Canada. Newman's troubled past, including a track record of attention-seeking, would culminate in him becoming the subject of the largest manhunt in the history of Montreal, which would eventually extend internationally.

The Early Years

Anna Yourk and Donald Newman, Luka's parents, separated when he was very young. Luka was the oldest of three children. He and his two younger sisters were sent to live with their grandparents.

Newman's high school teachers and classmates remembered him as self-obsessed about his looks. Newman dropped out of high school and began working as a stripper at a Toronto nightclub at the age of 19. He worked as an escort and appeared in pornographic videos, gay and straight.

Newman perpetrated his first crime in his early twenties. He won the trust of a woman with a mental handicap and persuaded her to apply for credit cards. Newman committed fraud by making charges on the cards that totaled $10,000. He was also suspected of sexually assaulting the woman.

The sexual assault charges were dropped due to medical reports that indicated Newman had a significant psychiatric issue. Instead, Newman was found guilty on four counts of fraud and received probation and community service. Looking back at the decision to drop the charges, Newman's defense attorney stated that this had changed the course of Newman's life, and the impact was "immeasurable, with huge ramifications for our society eventually."

Newman then began dating a transgender woman, who would later tell investigators that Newman wanted to be famous and would beg her to take pictures of him. She described his apartment as "looking like a shrine dedicated to himself." Their relationship lasted several months before they broke up. Shortly afterward, Newman changed his name to Luka Rocco Magnotta.

Starving for Attention

At age the age of 25, Magnotta auditioned for reality television shows in his continued effort to become famous. During an audition for one of the shows, he told the judges, "Some people say I am devastatingly good-looking." Another show he auditioned for was *Plastic Makes Perfect*, which features contestants who have had plastic surgery. He told the judges, during his audition, "I've had my nose done. I've had two hair transplants...and I'm planning on having muscle implants in my pecs and my arms." Magnotta failed to make the cut for any of the shows.

When his efforts to get on television failed, Magnotta became heavily involved with social media, opening multiple accounts on Facebook and other platforms. He used accounts that were set-up under aliases to spread rumors about himself and then used accounts that were established under his real name to defend himself. His online efforts to promote himself took a disturbing turn in 2010 when he posted a video link to his Facebook page titled, '3 Guys 1 Hammer.'

The video showed a man being brutally beaten and killed. Magnotta did not have any involvement in the murder, but personalized the posting with the tag, "Luka is unable to live unless there is chaos in his life, it makes him feel as though he matters."

Just before Christmas that year, he posted a second video called, '1 Guy-2 Kittens.' The video showed an unidentified man (his face was not visible) using a vacuum cleaner to suck the air out of a plastic bag that contained two kittens.

Outrage over the kitten video led to the formation of Facebook groups, whose mission was to locate Magnotta and bring him to justice. The groups collaborated with law enforcement, but their efforts yielded minimal results during their first year of investigation.

Magnotta's online activity was rampant in early 2012, as he posted countless blogs about necrophilia and sedatives. Toward midyear, an online promotion for a yet-to-be-released video titled, '1 Lunatic 1 Ice Pick' surfaced. The animal rights groups looking for Magnotta believed he was responsible for this video as well.

Reaching the Tipping Point

On May 25th, just a few days after the promotional video had been released, the full-length video of '1 Lunatic 1 Ice Pick' appeared online. The eleven-minute video opened with a shot of a naked male tied to a bed frame. The person operating the video camera, who is not visible to the viewer, violently attacks the restrained man by repeatedly stabbing him, first with an ice pick and then with a kitchen knife. Toward the end, the assailant removes a piece of flesh from his victim and feeds it to a dog.

On May 29th, the receptionist on the 12th floor of the Conservative Party's headquarters received a package. She started to open it but became suspicious when she noticed bloodstains and detected a putrid smell. Staffers called the Ottawa Police Department, who responded with a Hazmat crew. When they opened the package, they found a human foot.

Two elementary schools, St. George School and False Creek Elementary School, both received similar packages on June 5th. The St. George package contained a right foot, while the package sent to False Creek contained a right hand. The packages were sent from Montreal, where Magnotta was living.

Around the same time, other packages showed up containing body parts. A package containing a left hand was located at the processing facility of the Canadian Post Office; the package was addressed to Canada's Liberal Party. On May 25th, a janitor for an apartment building in Montreal noticed a suitcase in the building's alley. Inside it, he found a badly decomposed torso.

The Investigation

Police interviewed residents in the area where the torso was found, looking for possible clues. While conducting their interviews, they learned that Magnotta had an apartment nearby. Police went to his apartment, but the apartment manager informed them that Magnotta had recently moved. When the manager let the police into the now-vacated apartment, they found bloodstains on a mattress and table that Magnotta had left behind. They also found bloodstains in the bathtub.

Police discovered the following message written in red ink on the inside of a cupboard door, "If you don't like the reflection. Don't look in the mirror. I don't care." They then viewed the video from the apartment's security camera. The video showed an individual resembling Magnotta carrying out a large number of garbage bags.

On May 30th, 2012, detectives got a hit on the identification of the body parts; they belonged to Lin Jun, a Chinese national, who was attending Concordia University in Montreal. On July 1st, Jun's decapitated head was found by a visitor at the edge of a lake in Angrignom Park in Montreal.

The Montreal Police issued an arrest warrant for Magnotta, which was later upgraded to an arrest warrant applicable throughout Canada. Magnotta faced charges including first-degree murder, committing an indignity to a dead body, the publishing of obscene material, mailing obscene, indecent, immoral, or scurrilous material, and criminally harassing the Canadian Prime Minister and several members of parliament.

A Red Notice was issued by Interpol on May 31st, 2012, and Magnotta's photograph was posted on the Interpol website. The Red Notice gave any Interpol member state permission to arrest Magnotta pending extradition back to Canada.

Unbeknownst to Montreal authorities, Magnotta had flown to Paris, May 25th, using his own passport. After the Interpol Red Notice was issued, Paris officials were able to track his movement by following his cell phone signal. They tracked him to a hotel in the city of Bagnolet; however, he had left by the time police arrived. Authorities found pornographic magazines in his hotel room.

From Paris, Magnotta flew to Berlin, Germany. On June 4th, Berlin police located Magnotta in an internet café in Neukolln, a district of Berlin, where he was reading the latest news about himself. Magnotta appeared in a Berlin court, June 5th, and was ordered to be extradited to Canada. A preliminary hearing was held in a high-security Montreal courtroom on March 11th, 2013.

On Trial

Magnotta elected to have a trial by jury and pleaded not guilty. He did not deny that he had done everything that he was charged with but claimed diminished responsibility due to mental disorders.

The prosecutor argued that Jun Lin's murder was organized and premeditated, saying that Magnotta was "purposeful, mindful, ultra-organized, and ultimately responsible for his actions."

Magnotta's attorney offered evidence that his client had been diagnosed with paranoid schizophrenia when he was a teenager. A psychiatrist for the defense, Dr. Joel Watts, testified that Magnotta showed symptoms of borderline personality disorder, histrionic personality disorder, and episodic schizophrenia. The prosecutor argued the symptoms described by the defense expert were the result of Magnotta's drug use as a teenager.

Magnotta did not testify during the 12-week trial. The jury began deliberations on December 15th, 2014, and by December 23rd, they found Magnotta guilty on all charges. He received a mandatory life sentence, plus an additional 19 years for related charges. Though Magnotta filed an appeal, claiming judicial error during jury instructions, he later withdrew it.

There are many people in society who feel isolated from others and hungry for attention. When we act indifferently toward others, some of these people will raise the stakes until they get noticed. Magnotta was one such individual.

IV
Shari Tobyne

ARIZONA IS KNOWN FOR ITS EXTREME HEAT; THE seasons of fall and winter bring temperatures that are much more pleasant. Outdoor enthusiasts take full advantage of the weather and the natural beauty of the Copper State at that time of year. Unfortunately, such pleasures were not awaiting a group of outdoor adventurers in December 2010.

The Disbursement of Body Parts

While hiking in Pinal County, some individuals came across a gruesome discovery. They found human remains off U.S. Highway

60, just south of Florence Junction. The remains were sent to the Pinal County Medical Examiner's Office in Tucson.

On December 23rd, hikers in La Paz County found body parts off Interstate 10, near mile marker 53, just 50 miles from the California border. The remains were sent to the Pima County Medical Examiner's Office.

On December 26th, a driver on the Beeline Highway spotted partial human remains off the side of the road near the Sugarloaf off-ramp. Those remains were sent to the Maricopa County Medical Examiner's Office.

A Family's Concern

Five months earlier, the adult children of 57-year-old-Dwight Tobyne contacted the Scottsdale Police Department. They were concerned about their father's welfare, as they had lost contact with him. He had not shown up for Christmas or the birth of his grandchild. Their mother, Shari Tobyne, had told her children their father had gone to Mexico and would be returning in late November.

Detectives visited Shari Tobyne at her condominium in the 8000 Block of East Mountain View Road. During their interview, detectives became suspicious of Shari, as she was unable to answer their questions directly. As a result, they placed her under surveillance.

They observed her placing a large trash bag in the dumpster behind a store in Chandler, Arizona. When the trash bag was recovered, police found a gun and pieces of clothing inside. Later, they observed Tobyne visiting a self-serve car wash, where she spray-cleaned the trunk of her car.

Tobyne was arrested and brought to the Scottsdale Police Department for further questioning. At the time, the Scottsdale Police were not aware that the Arizona Department of Public Safety crime lab had determined that the human remains found in the three different counties belonged to the same individual.

Eliminating Hubby

During the August 14th interview, Tobyne told detectives she had bought the gun with the intention of using it to kill herself. She divulged that her husband, Dwight, had advised her he was leaving her and moving back to Oklahoma, after 35 years of marriage. Tobyne described Dwight's death as follows: she walked into their bedroom with the gun pointed at her head, but when Dwight jumped up from bed to grab it from her, the gun accidentally went off, killing him.

Tobyne feared no one would believe it was an accident, so she wrapped up Dwight's body in a tarp, placed him in her car, and dumped his body in the Tonto Forest, along the Bush Highway.

She also stated she replaced the master bedroom carpet due to the blood spatter. When Tobyne took investigators to the location where she claimed to have dumped the body, they found no trace of human remains.

As detectives continued their investigation, they found additional evidence that contradicted the statements Tobyne made during the first interview. For example, they uncovered the story Tobyne told her children about their father leaving her and going to Mexico in late November. Dwight and Shari's cell phone records showed both cell phones had been in the Phoenix area between November 24th and December 25th. Police also learned Tobyne had bought a handgun in early November and had taken shooting lessons. Further, Dwight Tobyne's truck had been found parked at a Phoenix apartment complex, near 30th Street and Shea Avenue. The doors were locked, the keys were in the ignition, and the battery was dead.

Detectives talked to the owner of the Tobyne's condominium on Mountain View, from whom the Tobyne's had been renting. The owner confirmed that Shari Tobyne had replaced the bedroom carpet, and the garage smelled strongly of bleach.

During their second interview with Tobyne, detectives confronted her with the new evidence. She confessed to killing her husband because he was leaving her. She had shot him on November 24th, 2009, the day before he planned to leave for Oklahoma. No one knew he was dead because she used his phone and e-mail account to send messages to friends and family to avoid suspicion.

Charges and Prosecution

The charges against Tobyne for first-degree murder would be challenging to prove because authorities still did not have a body. According to the district attorney in the Tobyne case, the pursuit of a murder charge without a body had been achieved successfully before, but such cases were rare. He could remember only two or three instances in Phoenix where there was a prosecution without a body within the last 25 years.

On October 7th, 2010, detectives finally received news that the human remains found in the three counties all had come from the same individual. Detectives were able to get a DNA sample from Dwight Tobyne's father, who lived in Kansas. His DNA sample was a close enough match to determine the human remains belonged to Dwight Tobyne.

Tobyne was sentenced to life in prison on May 19th, 2013. She received an additional 31 years for related charges.

V

David Michael Barnett

"I JUST SNAPPED." THESE WERE DAVID BARNETT'S chilling words to the reporter interviewing him.

Barnett's story is one of heinous violence and a challenge to the death penalty. Barnett was born May 18, 1976, in Glendale, Missouri. He grew up in a severely dysfunctional home. His father was a violent alcoholic, and his mother made frequent attempts to abandon David. After David was born, his mother tried to leave the hospital without him and later tried to leave him with a drug-addicted sex worker.

By the age of five, Barnett had been removed from his parent's home and placed in a series of foster homes. His grandparents eventually adopted him. By eight years old, Barnett was contemplating suicide. He survived an overdose on prescription drugs in his late teens.

Deadly Sunday

Barnett's fateful day was Sunday, February 4, 1996, at 8:00 a.m. His grandparents were attending a service at the Kirkwood Baptist Church. Barnett, twenty at the time, was spending more and more time living with his friends, as he was not getting along with his grandparents. His grandparents were frustrated with him due to his delinquent behavior.

That terrible morning, Barnett walked back from his friends' house to his grandparents' home. When he arrived, he entered the house through the bedroom window. He lay down on the living room couch and fell asleep watching television.

His grandparents returned from church around 1:00 p.m. They were upset to find he had entered the home. An argument ensued and Barnett shoved his grandmother, causing her to fall to the floor. She lay there helplessly as her grandson violently shoved her husband. With both his grandparents on the floor, David made his way into the kitchen and grabbed a knife on the table.

He returned to the living room and stood over his dazed and confused grandparents. They could not believe what was happening to them. Barnett kicked his grandfather in the head as he struggled to get up. He stabbed his grandfather savagely a total of ten times to the head and hands. His grandfather's blood drained out of his dying body and covered the living room rug. When he was sure his grandfather was dead, Barnett returned to the kitchen to get another knife.

Returning to the living room, he headed for his grandmother. With rage still coursing through his veins, he stabbed her in the neck. The anger that he felt for his grandmother remained, despite the fact she lay dying. He returned to the kitchen yet again and returned with two new knives. He continued to stab her in the neck and face. By the time he was done, Barnett's grandmother had 12 stab wounds to her neck.

With his grandparents dead on the living room floor, Barnett hid the knives, placing one between the mattresses of his grandparent's bed. He washed the blood off his hands in the bathroom and headed for the garage. Barnett previously told his friends how much he wanted his grandfather's car, a 1995 Dodge Intrepid. He knew where his grandfather kept the keys, which he grabbed. He also took $120 from his grandmother's purse before driving away in the Intrepid.

Surrender

Police discovered the dead bodies of Barnett's grandparents by the next morning and commenced a search of the area. They found the stolen Intrepid in a nearby residential neighborhood. As they were inspecting the car, Barnett approached them and confessed to the murders.

The jury in Barnett's trial found him guilty, and he was convicted of two counts of first-degree murder. Prosecutors sought the death penalty during the sentencing phase, but Barnett's attorney asked for leniency, stating the Barnett suffered from post-traumatic stress, bipolar disorder, and depression. He also pointed to Barnett's childhood, which he described as "unstable." The jury deliberated for two days and decided on the death penalty.

Barnett appealed the death penalty decision, stating his attorney had failed to present information about the abuse and neglect he had experienced during his childhood. His appeal was denied; however, Judge E. Richard Webber ruled in Barnett's favor, stating that during the trial, there was no mention of Barnett's violent and alcoholic father, that Barnett had been sexually abused, nor any mention that his mother had made numerous attempts to abandon him.

In Webber's words, "at least one juror would have determined the balance of aggravating and mitigating circumstances did not warrant death in Mr. Barnett's case." Webber made the determination the attorney general could appeal the case if they wanted to pursue the death penalty, or Barnett would be sentenced to life in prison without parole. The latter eventually became Barnett's sentence.

Every child is like a sponge; they absorb the emotions given off by those around them. Children retain the energy from these emotions, and it becomes part of them. Barnett's story is an example of how family violence and neglect can destroy lives.

VI

Arunya Rouch

ARUNYA ROUCH SAT STOICALLY NEXT TO HER defense attorney in a St. Petersburg, Florida, courtroom. She didn't show any hint of emotion as trial proceedings came to a close. Nor did she react as friends and family members tearfully addressed her with their victim impact statements, nor when the jury of nine women and three men found her guilty of murder. It took the jury seven hours of deliberation to reach their verdict, a surprise to most who had predicted the deliberations would be over much sooner. Not a peep when the judge gave her a life sentence.

Going Back to The Beginning

Arunya Rouch was born in Thailand, where she lived in poverty. Looking for a better life, she moved to the United States and gained citizenship. She worked at Publix in Tarpon Springs, an employee-owned grocery store chain, along with her husband, Tom Rouch.

Rouch was a trainer for the company and in charge of opening seafood departments in new stores. On March 30th, 2010, Arunya Rouch, 41, was fired from Tarpon Springs Publix for making threats to a coworker who had planned to report Rouch for infringing company policy. Tarpon Springs Publix had a policy against working without clocking in first. The co-worker who planned to report Rouch was Gregory Janowski.

Grocery Store Shooting

Rouch left work upset with Janowski and other co-workers, whom she felt had disrespected her. At home, she grabbed a 9mm semiautomatic weapon and returned to work.

Upon arriving back at Tarpon Springs Publix, she saw Janowski sitting in his car in the parking lot. Rouch approached the parked car, took aim, and fatally shot him. Janowski slumped forward; his blood dripped onto the car seat and floor, forming a pool. Rouch then ran toward Tarpon Springs Publix. She was going to shoot her manager and the co-workers who had disgraced her.

Entering the building, she made her way toward her manager's office. The sight of a gun-toting Rouch instantly generated panic in the crowded store. Chaos broke out as shoppers screamed, dropped their groceries, and fled for their lives. People were trampling over each other as they rushed to the door.

A witness to the parking lot shooting had called 911. As the Tarpon Springs Police Department was just a block away from Tarpon Springs Publix, two officers arrived as Rouch entered the store. They rushed in the store and Rouch fired at them; a bullet grazed one of the officers. Rouch was able to get a few more shots off before one of the officers was able to shoot Rouch, wounding her. Police took Rouch to Bayfront Medical Center for treatment.

Motives and Sentencing

According to the FBI, Rouch was a rare case, as women commit only 5% of workplace homicides. Experts in workplace violence say that part of the reason for this low number is that women, unlike men, tend not to act violently in the workplace unless all other options fail. Further, when they do act violently, it is usually the result of long-term frustration, while men commit workplace violence to show they are in charge.

Rouch was married but did not have children, and she was a perfectionist at work. This rubbed many of her co-workers the wrong way. Those who knew her stated she loved her job and would often prepare food at home for her co-workers. Her husband, Tom Rouch, believed that she killed out of the sense she had disgraced her family by losing her job.

During Rouch's trial, her husband testified she had experienced chronic bullying by some of her co-workers and that management of Tarpon Springs Publix hadn't done anything to stop this. In his emotional testimony, Tom Rouch stated that his wife had been treated "like an animal" at work. He further stated that Janowski was the main culprit in the bullying and that in one incident, Janowski and other coworkers had locked Arunya in a seafood freezer.

Rouch had no history of mental illness and was found guilty of one count of first-degree murder, two counts of attempted first-degree murder, and two counts of aggravated assault.

Those who harass others do so because it gives them a sense of power. They pick a victim they feel is vulnerable, an easy target. When a target, like Arunya, reaches their breaking point, they may strike back in unexpectedly deadly ways.

VII

Brian Nichols

IN A 1992 COLLEGE ESSAY, BRIAN NICHOLS WROTE, "If violence can be a righteous tool for the white man, then surely it can be used as a righteous tool for the black man. If violence can be used to murder defenseless women and children in South Africa and Vietnam, then surely it can be used to defend the human rights of dark-skinned people all over the world."

He believed the white race had set out to eliminate black people by incarcerating black males to prevent them from breeding.

March 11th, 2005, Nichols backed up these words with actions by going on a brazen killing spree targeting the American justice system.

Background

Born December 10th, 1971, Brian Gene Nichols was raised in Baltimore, Maryland, by middle-class parents. He attended the University of Pennsylvania, where he played football and earned a reputation as someone not to mess with on or off the field. At 6'1" and 210 pounds, he was quite skilled in martial arts.

He frequently got into trouble and was arrested multiple times while at university. In 1990, alone, he was arrested for making terroristic threats, disorderly conduct and harassment, and assault regarding an incident in the university's dining hall. During his arraignment, Nichols pleaded guilty to disorderly conduct and harassment, and the remaining charges were dropped.

In 1995, deciding that school was not for him, Nichols quit and moved to Georgia. He worked a series of jobs, including Hewlett-Packard, UNIX Systems, and UPS, where he worked as a computer engineer and earned a six-figure income.

Holding on to the Past

Despite Nichols's professional success, his troubled past caught up with him when he turned his rage on an ex-girlfriend. He hadn't had contact with her in the previous eight years when he broke into her home, took her hostage at gunpoint, and raped her. Nichols was charged with rape, aggravated assault with the intent to rape, aggravated sodomy, false imprisonment, burglary, and the possession of a firearm during the commission of a crime.

His original trial for these offenses ended in a mistrial and a hung jury. The prosecution declared they would be applying for a re-trial. In response, Nichols announced to the crowded courtroom: "I'm not going to go lying down."

The retrial was scheduled for March 11th, 2005, until which time Nichols remained in custody. He backed up his announcement to the court, with those close to him warning authorities that he would attempt an escape. If he were found guilty at the retrial, Nichols would receive life in prison.

Assault on The Justice System

On the morning of his re-trial, sheriff's deputy Cynthia Hall, a petite 51-year-old woman, rode with Nichols to the courthouse in the sheriff department's bus. Hall was familiar with Nichols as she was frequently assigned to guard him. When the bus arrived at the courthouse, Hall escorted Nichols to a holding cell in the courthouse so he could change clothes in preparation for his trial.

During this process, Hall made two costly mistakes: 1) she didn't accept any assistance in transferring Nichols; and 2) she didn't put leg shackles on Nichols, which was standard practice.

When they reached the holding cell, Hall removed Nichols' handcuffs so he could change clothes. As soon as his hands were free, Nichols struck Hall hard in the face so hard she was lifted off the cement floor. Nichols viciously attacked Hall and shoved her into the holding cell. He removed her gun, gun magazine, and radio from her pummeled body. He also took her keys and used them to secure Hall in the cell. Then he changed into his civilian clothes and used the keys to unlock a lockbox from which he took a Beretta .40 caliber semi-automatic pistol.

The judge from Nichols' first trial, Judge Rowland W. Barnes, would oversee the re-trial as well. He was also Nichols' next target. While searching for Judge Barnes's chambers, Nichols came across case managers Susan Christy, Gina Clarke Thomas, and attorney David Allman. Nichols ordered them to the floor at gunpoint and demanded to know where Judge Barnes was located. While he was interrogating his captives, the court bailiff, Sergeant Grantley White, entered the room and attempted to disarm him. Nichols pointed his gun at his captives and cautioned Sergeant White, "Don't do anything, Sarge. I've got nothing to lose."

Nichols persuaded Sergeant White to drop his gun and ordered him to handcuff the three captives. Nichols did not realize that Sergeant White had pushed an emergency button on his radio. However, when security responded on White's radio, Nichols grabbed it, impersonating Sergeant White, told the caller their assistance was not needed, and had pressed the emergency button by accident. Nichols ordered his captives into a bathroom and continued his search of Judge Barnes.

Judge Barnes was in courtroom 8-F presiding over a civil trial. He did not see Nichols standing in the doorway behind him. Nichols had a clear, unobstructed view of Judge Barnes' back. Nichols took his time to check the courtroom for the Assistant District Attorneys involved in his re-trial, but they were nowhere to be seen. As it was a civil trial, the only court officials there were Judge Barnes and court reporter Julie Brandau. Nichols shot Judge Barnes in the back of the head and then shot Brandau. He then went to the courtroom where his re-trial was to be held and searched the witness waiting room. He was looking for his ex-girlfriend, the one who he had beaten and raped. Fortunately, the room was empty.

Nichols ran out of the courthouse through an emergency exit. A security officer, Sergeant Teasley, was just reporting to work when he encountered Nichols making his escape. Nichols shot Sergeant Teasley twice in the abdomen and ran off. Judge Barnes, Brandau, and Sergeant Teasley all died on arrival at Grady Memorial Hospital.

Nichols ran to a parking garage outside the courthouse. He carjacked a 2002 Mazda Tribute, belonging to a Sheriff Deputy who had just arrived for work. Larry McCrary, who worked in the juvenile court, happened to witness the carjacking and parked his car on the exit ramp so Nichols would not be able to drive out. He then went to an upper level of the parking garage to flag down any officers who might be in the area.

When Nichols realized the parking garage exit was blocked, he calmly got out of the car and walked out instead. He spotted a tow truck parked on the side of the street and carjacked it. In his rush to drive off in the tow truck, however, he drove the wrong way down a one-way street and was forced to enter another parking garage.

Nichols abandoned the tow truck and carjacked a 2004 Mercury Sable. Unlike the previous carjacking's where he had forced the victim out of the car, Nichols made the driver, Almeta Kilgo, move over to the passenger seat. Kilgo complied, and Nichols drove a few miles before pulling over in a secluded area. He ordered Kilgo to get in the trunk; however, she was able to escape when Nichols noticed some other people in the area and got distracted. Nichols took off in Kilgo's car, leaving her behind. Nichols carjacked two additional cars in his efforts to flee. One of the drivers was hit over the head with a gun and required stitches.

On March 12th, the Duluth Police Department received a call from a woman who was being held hostage by Nichols in her apartment. The woman, Ashley Smith, had been able to gain Nichol's trust, allowing her to get away long enough to call the police. When the police arrived at Smith's apartment, Nichols surrendered.

On May 5th, 2005, a Fulton County Grand Jury indicted Nichols on 54 counts, including murder, felony murder, kidnapping, armed robbery, aggravated assault, aggravated battery, theft, carjacking, and escape from authorities. The district attorney sought the death penalty, while Nichols's attorney argued for leniency due to his client's mental health. While waiting for his trial to start, Nichols made another attempt to escape but was unsuccessful. His trial was held on September 22nd, 2008, in the Atlanta Municipal Court. It concluded on December 23rd, 2008, where he was sentenced to multiple life sentences.

More money was spent on Nichols than any other defendant in Georgia's history, with the case costing over $3 million.

VIII

Valerie Pape

THE CASE OF VALERIE PAPE, FILLED WITH celebrities, politics, mystery, and murder, has all the makings of a Hollywood movie. On January 23rd, 2000, a delivery driver arrived at a Basha's grocery store in Mesa, Arizona, located at McDowell and Power Roads. The delivery driver observed something strange from a distance. A 1997 Jaguar, driven by a woman, pulled up to the store's dumpster and tossed a large object into it before driving away.

The delivery driver went to the dumpster to investigate and made a horrific discovery. Lying in the dumpster was a human torso, cut between the breast-line and the knees. The delivery driver notified the Mesa Police Department.

Getting Her Story Straight

Detectives were able to trace the Jaguar back to a Valerie Pape of Scottsdale, Arizona. A second witness identified her from a composite drawing. The 47-seven-year-old was a French citizen born in the city of Rennes. She was married to Ira Pomeranz and owned an upscale beauty salon in downtown Scottsdale. The police went to her Scottsdale home and took her to the police station for questioning.

She first told the police that she had come home to find her husband lying dead in a pool blood. She panicked and, not knowing what to do, decided to go to work at her beauty salon. When she returned from work, she dumped his body behind the Basha's grocery store, fearful that she would be blamed for his murder. Pape did not respond to questions regarding the body's dismemberment.

Detectives searched Pape's home and found evidence that contradicted her story. They found a receipt in her purse for a reciprocating saw she had purchased from a Scottsdale hardware store. They also found a bullet under the rear seat of her Jaguar.

When presented with the evidence, Pape changed her story and confessed to shooting her estranged husband. She told the detectives that she and her husband had been involved in a domestic dispute when she shot him. She had dumped his body four days later.

She continued to deny any knowledge of how his body was dismembered. Given that Pape was a petite woman, detectives were positive she must have had an accomplice. Meanwhile, the media was following the case closely, referring to it as the "Torso Murder" case.

At her hearing in the Superior Court of Maricopa County, Pape pled guilty to killing her estranged husband. Her attorney claimed the killing was the result of a domestic dispute they'd had on January 23rd, 2000. In investigating Pape and Pomerantz's history, the Attorney General discovered past records of domestic disputes and restraining orders.

Political Friends

Additional investigations into Pape's background led to further intrigue. The beauty salon that Pape owned also had an art gallery that displayed the work of local artists. One of those artists was Rusty Bowers, a state senator from the city of Mesa. Bowers found it incomprehensible that Pape could have killed or dismembered her husband. In his words, "She is a very gentle, decent person, and I'm astonished at this."

Bower's administrative assistant was Merle Bianchi, who had been responsible for Pape meeting Bowers. Bianchi reaffirmed Bower's claim about Pape's character. Further, she said, Pape had shared with her that she was afraid of Pomerantz, relating to the detectives a time when Pape had called her and told her that Pomerantz had thrown knives at her during an argument. Bianchi had allowed Pape to stay with her. In Bianchi's words, Pape was "…the most kind, warmest, most gentle person you ever met in your life. She was naive and trusting."

In 1999, Bianchi's husband, Ron Bianchi, was found slain in the forests of Payson, Arizona. His killer was never found. Authorities from Gila County who were investigating the Bianchi murder followed the Pape investigation with interest.

A local newspaper, the Arizona Republic, ran an article that insinuated Ron Bianchi was murdered because he was investigating an affair between Senator John McCain and singer Connie Stevens. Because there was a lack of any evidence to support the article, it was dismissed.

The Sentencing

As a result of their findings, the district attorney was convinced that Pape did not act with premeditation and charged Pape with second-degree murder. On August 20th, Pape agreed to a plea deal whereby she did not have to reveal who dismembered her husband's body if she agreed to plead guilty to second-degree murder.

On November 7th, the Arizona State Prison placed Pape in the custody of U.S. Marshals Service. She was to be delivered to a federal transfer center in Oklahoma City in preparation for being turned over to the French police. The director of the Arizona Department of Corrections, Dora Schiro, approved the move. The international transfer was dropped when Pomerantz's daughter expressed her concern the French would release Pape on parole.

Subsequently, Pape was sentenced to 16 years without parole in an Arizona prison.

IX

Robert Bever

DESPITE BEING THE LARGEST SUBURB IN TULSA, Broken Arrow has the lowest crime rate of any city in Oklahoma. Its crime rate is 66% lower than the surrounding areas.

However, that sense of peace was shattered on July 22nd, 2015, around 11:30 p.m. In a panicked state, a 12-year-old girl called 911. She said her brother was killing her family. The 911 dispatcher could hear screaming and yelling in the background, as well as an older male voice. Before the operator could get any information from the caller, the phone went dead. The dispatcher was able to track down the address, and the police were sent to 709 Magnolia Court.

Massacre on Magnolia Court

When the police arrived at the house, they noticed blood on the porch and heard a faint voice from within. The officers drew their guns and cautiously entered the home. Inside, they found the aftermath of a bloody massacre. Lying on the floor in front of them was a 13-year-old girl. She was later identified as Crystal Bever. Her throat had been slit and she had multiple stab wounds to her stomach and arms. There was an adult male, later identified as 52-year-old David Bever. The father of the family, he had over 28 stab wounds to his face, neck, torso, and arms. Next to David's body, police found his wife, 44-year-old April Bever. She had experienced blunt force trauma and had over 48 stab wounds to her head and all over her body. Nearby were the bodies of their sons, 12-year-old Daniel, 7-year-old Christopher Bever, and 5-year-old daughter, Victoria Bever. Daniel had received nine stab wounds to his back, shoulder, and chest. Christopher had six stab wounds to his chest, back, shoulder, and lower leg. Victoria had 18 stab wounds to her neck, chest, back, and upper arm. Police found 2-year old Autumn Bever, alone and unharmed, huddling in the corner of her room.

Autumn Beaver was rushed to a nearby hospital where she was listed in serious but stable condition. Detectives discovered that it was Crystal who had placed the 911 call. When she was sufficiently recovered to be able to speak, she identified her two brothers; 18-year-old Robert and 16-year old Michael as the perpetrators of the deadly attack.

Family Secrets

Crystal told the officers when they had arrived on the scene, Robert and Michael had run out of the house through the back door. The brothers hid in a heavily wooded area next to their property and the police used their canine unit to locate them. Police arrested the two brothers and brought them to the Broken Arrow police station. The interviews with Robert, Michael, and Crystal that followed painted a picture of a severely dysfunctional family ripe for bearing such hateful fruit as these two young killers.

Crystal informed detectives that David Bever, her father, was frequently both verbally and physically abusive toward all of the children. She said that, more than once, David had "[thrown] them across the room" when he was angry and that he was especially hard on Robert and Michael. She also related a time when she had seen David beat her mom and slam her head against the wall.

The family lived in isolation from the rest of the community. The children were homeschooled and not allowed to interact with other children. They were so isolated that many of the neighbors only learned of the family members' names when they were released by the medical examiner.

Crystal also advised the detectives that Robert and Michael had spent the last year talking about killing their family and taking their parents' money. She indicated that both brothers were fascinated with mass shooters and always wanted to see such perpetrators avoid police capture. The brothers' philosophy was that there were too many people in the world, so they needed to kill as many as they could.

During their interview with Robert Bever, detectives learned that his parents were "hateful and abusive" toward him and his siblings and that both he and Michael had been planning to kill their parents since Robert was 13. He explained how he'd gotten a job working in a call center so he could save enough money to buy guns, bullets, knives, and body armor. He would order the weapons online and have them delivered to a local gun shop, where he would pick them up.

In fact, he had ordered ammunition on the day of the attack. Detectives found 3,000 rounds of ammunition the brothers ordered. Michael and Robert had planned to kill their family, cut up and dismember them, and place their parts in plastic storage containers they would hide in the attic. The brothers had intended to kill their two-year-old sister but had to flee when the police arrived.

Robert further explained that if the police had not arrived, they would have continued their killing spree as they drove across the country. They wanted to kill 100 people. He confirmed what Crystal had told the detectives: that he respected serial killers and mass shooters. To Robert, killing multiple people would make him "God-like." He believed that if he killed enough people, those who were not contributing to society would eventually be eliminated.

Sentencing

Both brothers were charged with five counts of first-degree murder and one count of assault and battery with the intent to kill. Their crime is considered the "worst single criminal event in Broken Arrow history."

Robert pled guilty to all counts and was sentenced to life in prison without the possibility of parole.

Michael Bever was found guilty of the charges and sentenced to five life sentences plus twenty-eight years for the assault.

The surviving children were placed in foster homes.

No child is born evil. When children commit evil, it is because they have experienced evil; often from the very ones who are supposed to protect them.

Michael Bever was a time bomb waiting to explode.

X
Amy Bishop

IN MARCH 2008, AMY BISHOP, A BIOLOGY professor at the University of Alabama, was in her office catching up on her mail before her next class started. She didn't know it at the time, but she was about to open one particular piece of mail that would trigger a chain of events leading to the death of three people. The letter was from the Dean of the Colleges of Science and stated that Bishop was being dismissed from the university as of February 26th, 2010. Bishop was advised that the spring of 2010 would be her last semester at the university, as she had not made tenure.

Background

From an outsider's view, Bishop appeared to be a success in life. Born April 24th, 1965, Bishop was married, had four children, and highly educated.

She received her undergraduate degree from Northeastern University in Boston, earned her Ph.D. in genetics from Harvard University, and became an assistant professor at the University of Alabama in 2003.

She also partnered with her husband in developing a portable cell incubator, a technology that maintains and supports the growth of microorganisms when conducting biological experiments. Their endeavors were part of a competition in which they won third place and $25,000.

Bishop is the second cousin of author John Irving. When she was living in Massachusetts in the 1990s, she had also pursued writing by joining the Hamilton Writer's Group. She hoped that becoming a writer would allow her to leave academia. She wrote three novels, none of which were ever published. Despite her accomplishments, there were problems with her conduct.

Members of the Hamilton Writer's Group have stated that she tried to present herself as a serious writer by frequently bringing up her degree from Harvard and her association with John Irving. They also found her to be abrasive and self-righteous and deemed herself deserving of praise. In her tenure review meeting at the University of Alabama, Bishop learned that one of her colleagues on the board had referred to her as "crazy." In response, Bishop filed a complaint with the Equal Employment Opportunity Commission.

During faculty meetings, some professors accused her of acting erratically. She was not popular with her students, who saw her as a poor instructor. They felt she was "ineffective in the classroom and behaved in odd and unsettling ways." Some of her students went so far as to sign a petition requesting the University take action, but nothing ever came of it. Bishop once published an academic article and used the names of her husband and children as the article's co-authors.

According to the University, Bishop did not receive tenure because she had not submitted all her research papers in time to get published, so they did not count toward her tenure. The University board also felt she was spending too much time seeking patents for her portable cell incubator. However, there were darker parts of Bishop's past of which the University was unaware.

In 1986, Bishop fatally shot her brother; however, no charges were brought as it was ruled to be an accident. In 1993, both she and her husband were suspected of sending a letter bomb to Paul Rosenberg, a colleague of Bishop at Harvard University. The letter bomb failed to explode, and authorities lacked the evidence required to bring charges against the Bishops. In 2002, Bishop was charged with misdemeanor assault and disorderly conduct for punching another customer at the International House of Pancakes in Peabody, Massachusetts.

Tragic Meeting

The same morning that Bishop received her letter of termination, February 26th, 2010, she was scheduled to attend a faculty meeting for the biology department. The meeting started around 3:00 p.m. and attended by twelve of her colleagues, who sat around a large oval meeting table. Bishop sat silently as the group discussed business. After 40 minutes had passed, Bishop stood up and pulled out a 9-mm handgun. She shot the person sitting next to her in the head and then methodically shot each person around the table in the head. Those who were sitting on the opposite side of the table attempted to take refuge on the floor.

In the words of Debra Moriarity, a survivor of the attack, "This wasn't random shooting around the room; this was execution-style." Moriarity survived because Bishop's gun jammed when it was her turn.

With the help of others, Moriarity rushed Bishop and pushed her out of the room before barricading the door. Bishop had killed three people and wounded three others.

September 11th, 2012, she was charged with three counts of capital murder and three counts of attempted murder.

She was sentenced to life in prison without the possibility of parole and being incarcerated at the Julia Tutwiler Prison for Women. While in prison, Bishop was hospitalized after she attacked another female inmate.

XI

Bryan Uyesugi

A XEROX REPAIRMAN COMMITTED THE WORST mass murder in Hawaii's history and one of the worst workplace shootings in U.S. history.

Born in 1959 (exact date unknown) in Honolulu, Bryan Uyesugi lived in a section of the island known as Nuuanu. His home life was unremarkable and he joined the Army JROTC while he attended Roosevelt High School.

Those who knew him remember him as a quiet boy who never got into trouble. Uyesugi had two main interests, which became his hobbies; Koi, which he raised and bred, and collecting firearms. He owned 25 guns, all registered in his name.

Life-Changing Events

Those who knew Uyesugi point to three events in his life that changed him for the worst.

The first event was a car accident he was involved in after graduating high school in 1997. He crashed his father's car, hitting his head against the windshield. His family reported that he was never the same after the accident. The second event was when he was hired at Xerox in 1984, and the third event was the death of his mother in 1988. It was around this time that Uyesugi started experiencing painful sensations in his head.

Job Stress

Uyesugi worked as a technician at Xerox for over 15 years. He worked at the Nimitz warehouse for most of that time. His co-workers considered him very knowledgeable about his job but commented that while he never missed work, they felt he lacked social skills and did not handle stress well.

His lack of ability to handle stress became evident when Xerox started phasing out the model of copier Uyesugi had always worked. Uyesugi resisted every attempt by management to get him to attend training for the new copier model. He was concerned he would not be able to keep up with this change in technology.

On November 1st, Uyesugi was advised he must start training the very next day. Uyesugi felt cornered; if he did not attend training, he would be fired.

Besides being required to go to training, Uyesugi was transferred to a different workgroup. The culmination of these work changes led Uyesugi to believe the company was out to get him. He made unfounded accusations against other employees, saying they were harassing him and tampering with the product. Some of his team members ostracized him, causing him to feel withdrawn and isolated. These feelings led him to make threats against some of his co-workers.

Background

Uyesugi's first encounter with the law was in 1985 when he was found guilty of driving under the influence. His driver's license was suspended. He was sentenced to 72 hours of community service and fined $200.

In 1993, Uyesugi was arrested for third-degree criminal property damage for kicking an elevator door. He was ordered to attend an anger management course and undergo a psychiatric evaluation.

Psychological History

Uyesugi did see a psychiatrist, who concluded that he was suffering from deep-rooted delusions. As a result, Uyesugi spent five days at Castle Hospital for observation. Uyesugi told Dr. Mee-Lee, the psychiatrist in charge of his case there, that he had experienced auditory and visual hallucinations. He spoke of voices he heard in his head and black shadows that followed him.

Dr. Mee-Lee felt that Uyesugi was suffering from delusional disorder and paranoia. He also disclosed that he had thoughts about conducting a mass shooting. Uyesugi would later confide to his brother that he saw 'shadows' and they were trying to pin him down.

In 1997, Uyesugi's father, Hiro, had a Shingon priest bless their home. He hoped it would help relieve his son's fears; however, the priest advised Hiro that he suspected that Uyesugi was experiencing mental illness. Uyesugi's father urged his son to get psychiatric help, but he refused.

The Day of the Shooting

On November 2nd, 1999, Uyesugi reported to work as usual. His father would later say he seemed perfectly normal. He arrived at Xerox at 8:10 a.m. and was scheduled to attend a meeting with his work team to discuss concerns about his productivity.

He entered the building and took the elevator to the second floor. Upon reaching the second floor, he pulled out a 9mm Glock and started firing into the offices as he made his way down the hall. Four of the seven employees that Uyesugi killed were members of his own team.

Other employees were working in the warehouse, located at the rear of the building. When they heard the shots, some of them came to investigate what was happening. They did not know the sound they had heard was gunfire. One of those employees was George Moad, who testified in court about his experience encountering the bloody dead bodies of his co-workers. "I saw bodies and I couldn't understand, fathom…" he testified. "I felt sick."

Another employee escaped being Uyesugi's eighth fatality by running down a stairwell when he realized what was happening.

Though Uyesugi fired at him, he missed his target. The victims were Christopher Balatico, age 33, Ford Kanehira, age 41, Melvin Lee, age 58, Peter Mark, age 46, Ronald Kataoka, age 50, and John Sakamoto, age 36.

After the massacre was over, Uyesugi stole a green company van and drove off. Parking attendant Edith Nakamura, who saw Uyesugi leave the building and drive away, would later say, "He wasn't speeding. He just drove past calmly."

The Capture

Uyesugi drove to the Hawaii Nature Center, located in Makiki. The manhunt closed in on him there when police received intelligence about his location. The Hawaii Nature Center is in an area of the island that is densely populated, with several schools nearby. While the manhunt was on, Hanahauoli School was locked down and teachers kept students inside; the same occurred at Montessori Community School. Additionally, ten homes were evacuated.

The police cordoned off a half-mile around Uyesugi, who was sitting in the parked van. A SWAT team used a bullhorn to communicate with Uyesugi in what became a five-hour stand-off. Uyesugi gave up and surrendered around 3:00 p.m.

Trial, Sentencing, and Lawsuits

Uyesugi had his preliminary hearing on November 6th, 1999. He pleaded innocent to one count of first-degree murder and seven counts of secondary murder. A first-degree murder charge in Hawaii covers multiple killings and carries a mandatory sentence of life imprisonment without the possibility of parole. Uyesugi was held on $7 million bail.

Uyesugi's trial began on May 15th, 2000. The psychiatrist for the defense argued that Uyesugi was not guilty due to reason of insanity, as his client feared there was a conspiracy going on among his co-workers to get him fired. The prosecution's psychiatrist argued that while Uyesugi had schizophrenia, he was angry that he was facing termination of employment due to insubordination. Further, the prosecution argued, Uyesugi demonstrated he knew what he was doing when committing the massacre.

On June 13th, 2000, the 12-person jury found Uyesugi guilty on all charges, taking only two hours for deliberation. As Hawaii does not have the death penalty, Uyesugi was sentenced to life imprisonment without the possibility of parole on August 8th.

Uyesugi appealed his conviction to the Hawaii Supreme Court in 2002, arguing that he'd had inadequate representation during his first trial.

In 2005, both Xerox and Castle Hospital, who had evaluated Uyesugi, settled a lawsuit brought by the victims' families. The families argued that both Xerox and Castle were negligent in failing to protect society from Uyesugi's instability, noting that Uyesugi's violent tendencies were known as far back as 1993.

Additionally, the Hawaiian state legislature passed a law that requires medical professionals to provide information on the mental state of those who are applying for the purchase of a gun.

In June, the Supreme Court ruled in favor of the prosecution, agreeing that Uyesugi was aware of his actions at the time of the crime. Uyesugi was imprisoned at the Tallahatchie County Correctional Facility, located in Tutwiler, Mississippi. Tallahatchie was chosen due to the inability of the Halawa Correctional Facility to isolate prisoners.

Society is like a fabric; each thread intersects with all the other threads. When the threads do not intersect with each other, the fabric falls apart. Xerox and Castle Hospital failed to do their due diligence, costing eight people their lives.

XII
Antoinette Renee Frank

THE CASE OF ANTOINETTE FRANK demonstrates the tragic consequences that can occur when an individual is given police powers while being completely unfit to carry them out.

A Department in Crisis

In the late 1990s, the New Orleans Police Department was at a crisis point. The department was experiencing a major turnover in officers due to the department's ineffectiveness. The pay scale for New Orleans police officers was lower than most cities of comparable size.

Further, there was widespread corruption and several officers had been arrested for committing crimes, including murder and selling of drugs.

The department had a requirement that they could only hire residents of New Orleans.

For Antoinette Frank, born April 30th, 1971, becoming a police officer was a childhood dream. She'd always wanted to be a police officer. Frank was accepted to the New Orleans police academy in the early 90s and graduated on February 28th, 1993. She was granted an interview with the New Orleans Police Department the same month.

It was at this point that the process broke down and the seeds of a nightmare were planted. In reviewing her job application, it became evident that Frank had made some untruthful statements. Further, several psychiatric evaluations concluded that she was not suitable for hire. Despite all this damning evidence, the New Orleans Police Department decided to hire her anyway, due to their shortage of officers. In addition, Frank was black, which they thought might be useful in the Department's attempts to reduce racial tensions.

While on the job, fellow officers had the impression that Frank lacked the confidence and decisiveness needed to be a police officer. She came off as weak and unsure. Some went as far as to say she made irrational decisions. After six months on the force, Frank's supervisor wanted her to go back to the academy for further training. However, he was faced with a severe shortage of officers, so instead, he opted to team her up with a veteran officer.

Pouring Gas on the Fire

The proverbial pouring of "gas on the fire" came when Frank encountered 18-year-old Roger Lacaze, a drug dealer who had been shot during an altercation with other dealers. Frank was assigned to take his statement. The line between professional conduct and emotional involvement dissolved as Frank and Lacaze quickly developed feelings for each other. What started off as a desire to help Lacaze get his life in order, soon developed into a sexual relationship. They were spending more and more time together, including when Frank was on the job.

Frank was not at all shy about her relationship with Lacaze and openly included him in her police work. She allowed him to ride with her while she was on duty and let him accompany her on police matters. She even introduced him to others as her "trainee" or as her nephew.

One of the places Frank frequented was Kim Anh Vietnamese restaurant, located on the east side of New Orleans. Frank used to do security work at the restaurant and had developed a friendly relationship with its owners. They often served her free food. It was for this reason that Frank took Lacaze to the restaurant on March 4th, 1995.

When Frank stopped doing security at Kim Anh Vietnamese restaurant, Ronald Williams replaced her. Williams was also on the force, in charge of scheduling the department's police officers, but was working security at the restaurant to supplement his income. Because of the low pay, many New Orleans police officers did security work on the side to make ends meet. When Frank and Lacaze arrived at the restaurant, Frank introduced Lacaze to Williams as her nephew. Williams did not fall for her lies. He recognized Lacaze as a drug dealer he had encountered in the past.

A Betrayal of Trust

It was midnight and the restaurant owner's daughter, 24-year-old Chau Vu, was helping her brothers, Quoc and Ha, and her sister

Cuong, to close the restaurant. Other than Williams and the Vu children, the restaurant was empty; except Frank and Lacaze. They had stayed past closing time, lingering to finish their meals and talk to Chau and her siblings. They finally left at 11 p.m.

Chau went to the kitchen to count the money and collect Officer William's payment for his services. It was then she noticed the key to the restaurant's front door was missing. She had last seen the key before letting Frank and Lacaze out of the restaurant. After they had left, she had locked the front door from the inside.

She paid Williams and mentioned to him that she was unable to find the key. Williams advised her that Lacaze was not Frank's nephew and that he could not be trusted. He explained to her about his past encounters with Lacaze. Suddenly, they heard someone at the front door demanding to be let in. Whoever was outside was banging and shaking the door. Chau rushed back to the kitchen and hid the money in a microwave oven before returning to the front of the restaurant.

She saw Quoc and Cuong talking to Williams. Suddenly the front door opened, and Frank entered the restaurant; she used the key she had stolen. Williams approached Frank to confront her about the key, but Frank completely ignored him and walked with determination toward the kitchen. As she passed Cuong and Quoc, she shoved them through the kitchen door and followed behind them.

Before Williams could do anything, the front door flew open: it was Lacaze. He had a 9mm pistol drawn and shot Williams in the back of the head. The bullet was shot at close range and severed William's spine, causing him to fall to the ground, unable to move. Lacaze fired two fatal shots, one at William's head and the other into his back. He then took William's service revolver and his wallet.

Distracted by the shooting, Frank left the kitchen and headed to the front of the restaurant. Chau used the opportunity to grab Quoc and Cuong and hid them inside the walk-in-cooler. She turned off the lights in the kitchen and hid inside a small storage space at the back of the kitchen. She did not know where Lacaze was.

Frank and Lacaze returned to the kitchen and searched desperately for the money, which they eventually found. Now that they had the money, Frank and Lacaze opened the door of the walk-in-cooler, forced Quoc and Cuong to their knees, and then shot them execution-style. They searched for Chau but were unable to find her. Fearing that their shots may have been heard from outside the restaurant, they took off.

Chau ran out of the restaurant to a neighboring business and used their phone to call 911. Unknown to Chau, Frank intercepted the 911 dispatcher's call and advised the dispatcher that she would respond to the shooting. When Frank arrived back at the restaurant, she ran toward Chau.

Fortunately for Chau, several police officers had arrived at the restaurant before Frank did. The other officers approached Frank before she could reach Chau. Frank acted innocently and asked what was happening and if Chau was all right. Chau was terrified and in disbelief that the person who had killed her siblings was now acting as though she wanted to help.

The officers sensed Chau's fear and told Frank not to leave. One of the officers took Chau aside and, in broken English, she told them what happened. Chau explained that Frank and Lacaze were the ones who had robbed the family's restaurant and murdered her brother and sister.

Interrogation and Trial

The police took Frank into custody and brought her to the station for interrogation. She told the detectives what had happened and even disclosed where she had dropped off Lacaze. Frank was charged and Lacaze was later picked up and taken into custody. They were interviewed separately, with each one implicating the other. Frank stated she shot Chau's siblings because Lacaze forced her to at gunpoint, while Lacaze claimed Frank was the mastermind behind the operation.

Frank and Lacaze were indicted by a grand jury on April 28th, 1995.

Lacaze's trial began July 17th, 1995 and lasted five days.

Frank's trial began on September 5th, 1995. The defense had subpoenaed 40 witnesses, yet not one of the witnesses was called to testify.

The jury deliberated for 22 minutes on September 12th, 1995, returning with a guilty verdict, which was a record for a capital murder case in the city of New Orleans. During the penalty phase, it took only 45 minutes for the jury to decide to give Lacaze the death penalty. Frank became the first police officer to be convicted of killing another police officer and was sentenced to death on October 20th, 1995.

Frank's attorney appealed to the Louisiana Supreme Court, arguing against the death sentence by presenting testimony from a psychiatrist who had evaluated Frank. The evaluation concluded Frank was suffering from trauma and diagnosed her with narcissistic personality disorder.

The Louisiana Supreme Court ruled Frank should face the death penalty as previously judged. Frank was sent to death row at the Louisiana Correctional Institute for Women, located near Baton Rouge. She was only the second woman in Louisiana's history to be sent to death row.

Noteworthy Discoveries

About two years before the murders at the Kim Anh Vietnamese restaurant, Frank's father, Adam Frank, disappeared and was reported missing. The last time he had been seen was at his daughter's home, where he had been staying. In November 1995, one month after Frank was found guilty, someone reported a foul smell coming from her home.

A canine-unit was sent in and the police found a human skull under the house. The skull had a bullet hole in it. It was identified as Adam Frank. Because Antoinette Frank was already facing the death penalty, no further charges were pursued.

During the trial, two witnesses testified that on February 4th, 1995, they had witnessed Frank and Lacaze engage in criminal activity unrelated to the shooting at the restaurant. The witnesses, John Stevens and Anthony Wallace, testified that Stevens had an altercation with Lacaze after leaving a party they had attended. Stevens was about to get into a fight with Lacaze, but Wallace convinced him to leave, and they did. Stevens and Wallace drove away in order to avoid a fight.

After a few minutes of driving, they were pulled over by a police car; the officer was Frank. Frank ordered both men out of their car. When they did, Wallace saw Lacaze holding a gun. Wallace charged at Lacaze and the two men got into a fight. When police back-up arrived, Frank told the officers that Wallace was the "bad guy" and that Lacaze was the "good guy." Wallace was arrested and charged with attempted murder and armed robbery.

As in the Uyesugi case, Frank is an example of what happens when the institutions that are supposed to serve us take short-cuts.

The New Orleans Police Department bestowed the power of the badge on to a tormented soul.

Conclusion

THERE IS A PARABLE ABOUT A MAN WHO IS hiking in the woods and comes across a river. As he is admiring the river, he sees another man drowning as he is carried downstream. The hiker jumps into the river and saves his life. The hiker continues to walk upstream, along the riverbank, where he encounters another man drowning in the river, fighting to stay afloat. Again, the hiker jumps into the river to rescue him. The hiker continues his journey upstream when he sees another man drowning in the river! The hiker rescues him and continues his hike. The hiker cannot believe it; he continues to encounter people drowning each time he moves further upstream.

When the hiker finally reaches the river's headwaters, he sees a bridge with a line of people on it. As he watches, he sees a man push one person at a time off the bridge and into the river. The hiker then realizes he could have saved so many more people if he had addressed the original cause of the problem, rather than dealing with the effects of the original cause.

The twelve murderers profiled in this book are like the drowning people, as are most – if not all – of the men and women who inhabit our jails and prisons. No baby is born into this world as an evil being. Rather, those people who we refer to as 'monsters' or murderers are a byproduct of society's failure to address core issues fundamental for the development of a healthy society.

As long as we fail to develop our compassion and marginalize those who we consider to be "different from us," we will continue to encounter drowning souls who are ready to lash out.

List of Twelve Volume 2

12 Terrifying True Crime Murder Cases

Introduction

SOME PEOPLE RESORT TO EXTREME MEASURES when they feel upset. After taking a fall, most of us brush ourselves off and move forward. Others go over the edge. In this book, you will read about how far some people will go when they have reached their lowest point. You will get a glimpse into the troubled lives of:

- Amateur filmmaker Blaine Norris, and friend, Ryan Trimble, who committed bloody murder for a film.
- James Holmes, who massacred movie-goers at an Aurora movie theater.
- Elliot Rodger, who terrorized a college town.

- Zachery Bowen, who dismembered his girlfriend and cooked her body parts.
- Byron Smith, who made a sport of killing two teenagers.
- David A. Burke, who took the passengers of an airline down with him.
- George Hennard, who committed mass murder at a Luby's restaurant.
- James Edward Pough, who became a mass shooter after his car was repossessed.
- Howard Unruh, who went on a killing rampage after his front gate was stolen.
- Angela Simpson, who tortured and murdered a man with a disability.
- Thomas Michael Lane, the student who terrorized a high school cafeteria.
- James Huberty, who carried out mass carnage at a McDonald's restaurant.

I
Blaine Norris and Ryan Trimble

THE MAKING OF THE FILM "THROUGH HIKE: A Ghost Story," was falling apart, as was the impassioned dream of its 25-year-old director, Blaine Norris.

Norris, a resident of Pennsylvania, was known for being a "horror movie geek," and a nerd. He was obsessed with making his first attempt at movie making a success. The last thing he wanted was to return to his job at Harrisburg Insurance Company, where he worked as a computer technician.

The Opening Scene

Norris camped out with a small group of amateur actors and actresses on the Appalachian Trail and began filming. The movie was about a group of young people hiking the Appalachian Trail, who gets murdered by the ghost of a coal-mining baron.

As the movie director, Norris had his friend and co-worker, Brian Trimble, who had his own equipment, film the scenes. An investor had put up $18,000 to complete the project; however, Trimble had put the project in peril by botching up the filming, causing the film to go over budget. The investor had withdrawn his money in frustration.

As the cast rested in their tents for the night, Norris stayed up and pondered his situation. He was feeling the stress of not being able to pay for the film. He had lost his investor, and his credit cards were maxed out. Even worse, he had borrowed against his house without telling his wife. She was already frustrated with him for spending all his time working on the movie.

As he sat by the campfire, Norris could no longer ignore the obvious. He was heavily in debt and had run out of money to complete the film. Feeling defeated, Norris realized that it was time to call it quits. He would gather his crew and return home the next morning. His lifelong dream had come to an end. That was all that he could think.

The next morning, Norris drove home to his apartment. He had moved there with his family when the bank foreclosed on their house. He entered the apartment and found it empty. Everything was gone, including the furniture. He spotted a note; from his wife. She explained that she could not take it anymore, and she was taking her son and moving on. Standing alone in the barren apartment, Norris came to the realization he had lost everything. He would have to return to his life as a computer technician; his dreams were not to be.

The Proposal and Rehearsal

The next day, Norris spent his lunch break with Trimble. Trimble confided with him about his own marital woes and Norris shared his hard-luck story as well. Trimble told Norris he was sick of married life and how his wife was constantly following-up on him. She always wanted to know where he was. He felt that his life was reduced to working to make his wife happy. This discussion resulted in the two men conspiring together to resolve their problems in a deadly manner.

Trimble shared with Norris that he had taken out a $100,000 life insurance policy on his wife. He asked Norris if he would be willing to kill her. In turn, he would pay Norris the money he needed to complete his film. Norris was interested. He thought about the idea of reviving his life's dream. Furthermore, his friend would be free of his wife.

Norris's desire to be a director kicked in. They spent the next few months planning the murder. He staged and repeatedly rehearsed the murder with Trimble, just as he had when directing his movie. On the day before the murder, Norris went to K-Mart and bought work gloves, a box of plastic surgical gloves, a hooded sweatshirt, and pants. He also bought a knife with a 6" blade.

Lights, Camera, Action, and Murder

On January 10, 2003, the plan was put into action. Trimble and his wife, Randi, lived in a townhouse in the city of Harrisburg. While Randi was at work, Norris entered the garage and waited for her.

As he waited, he could not help dreaming about his future as a movie director. He would have the insurance money to fund his film and make a major dent in his debt. Plus, he no longer had to put up with his wife's complaints. While Norris waited, Trimble was dining at a restaurant with friends. The dinner would provide Trimble with an alibi.

Norris heard a car pull up in the driveway; it was Randi. She got out of the car and went inside her home. She slipped out of her work clothes and lay down on the couch to relax. Norris slipped out of the garage, threw a metallic object against her car, and then hid in the shadows by the side of the garage.

As he hoped, Randi went to investigate. She inspected her car but did not notice anything suspicious. She turned around to make her way back to her front door. Unbeknownst to her, Norris had already made his way inside her home.

Norris lay in wait in the hallway. When Randi returned to the living room, he bided his time until she had turned her back to him. When she did, he pounced on her from behind. He put a rope around her neck and proceeded to choke her. Randi managed to place her fingers between the rope and her neck. Though she was choking, her fingers prevented Randi from killing her.

Frustrated, Norris cursed at her and stabbed her with his knife twenty-seven times. When he was done, Randi was completely covered in blood. Her hair was matted in it. Norris then ransacked the home to make the scene look like a burglary gone wrong.

The detectives were suspicious when they investigated the crime scene. It was clear to them that Randi's murder had not been the result of a robbery, as they could tell the ransacking had been staged. Eventually, Trimble confessed and agreed to testify against Norris to avoid the death penalty.

Because Norris agreed to confess, both men were sentenced to first-degree murder without the possibility of parole.

II
James Holmes

A CRISIS CENTER IN COLORADO RECEIVED A CALL on July 19, 2002. Earlier that same day, the same caller had made several attempts to reach a counselor but had been unsuccessful. To the caller's relief, he had finally made it through and was speaking to a crisis counselor. The caller started talking to the counselor but was disconnected after nine seconds. The individual who placed that call was James Holmes. He had called with the hope that someone could talk him out of committing what would later be referred to as the Aurora shooting massacre.

The Descent from Honor Roll to Darkness

Holmes was born December 13, 1987, in Oak Hills, California; his family moved to San Diego when he was twelve. As an adolescent, Holmes was withdrawn and spent much of his time playing video games. He was particularly fond of WarCraft III, where he was ranked among the top players. While he was socially awkward, he demonstrated strong academic achievement. In 2010, he graduated with honors from the University of California at Riverside, where he'd studied neuroscience. He was in the top one percent of his class and had a GPA of 3.949.

Holmes began working and then applied to graduate school. The Anschutz Medical Campus, located in Aurora, accepted him. This was the moment when his steady decline into darkness began. He found himself struggling academically for the first time in his life. Further, the girl he was dating; his first girlfriend was losing interest in him and just wanted to be friends. The stress of graduate school and the thought of losing his girlfriend were taking its toll.

The Holmes family had a history of mental illness. When he was younger, a therapist had recommended he take medication. He saw three different therapists at the university and shared with each of them that he was having homicidal thoughts. The therapists did not consider him a risk because he had not articulated a plan to carry out his thoughts.

Holmes became depressed and dropped out of graduate school, spending most of his time alone. The desire in him to harm others grew strong. He sent an email to the girlfriend, stating he had thoughts of killing others. He also sent his diary, which detailed his homicidal thoughts, to his former therapist. He wanted someone to stop him, to convince him there was another way. In a last-ditch attempt, he called the crisis line but was disconnected.

It was his sign. There was no turning back.

The Dark Knight and the Gunman

On July 20, Holmes armed himself with a Glock 22 pistol, Remington 870 Express Tactical shotgun, and a Smith & Wesson M&P 15 rifle. He also equipped himself with an urban assault vest, a gas mask, canisters of gas, and over 6,000 rounds of ammunition. He got into his car and drove to the Aurora Theater.

When he arrived at the theater, he parked his car and got out unarmed. He studied his surroundings as he walked to the theater. He purchased a ticket for the new Batman film, "The Dark Knight Rises," bought some popcorn, and sat down to watch the movie.

While the audience was focused on the movie, he was studying what was going on inside the theater and planning.

Halfway through the movie, Holmes left his seat and exited the theater. As he walked toward his car, he passed a line of 400 people waiting to buy tickets. There would be plenty of targets for his vengeance at the movies tonight.

He returned to his car and suited up. He put on his urban assault vest, armed himself with weapons, and put on the gas mask. Armed and ready, he walked toward the back of the theater and entered through an unlocked back door.

The audience did not notice Holmes right away as they were focused on the movie. He tossed two gas canisters in the center of the theater and immediately began shooting people. The crowd screamed, and chaos broke out. Most of the audience went diving to the floor, using the seats as shields. Some people in the back rows tried to run for the exits. The air was filled with smoke, the sound of gunfire, and lots of crying and screaming.

Suddenly, there was a strange silence; his rifle had jammed. The audience did not make a sound, hoping to avoid detection. The silence was short-lived: he grabbed the Glock 22 .40 caliber handgun and continued shooting. As the bullets sprayed the theater, some of them penetrated the walls and hit three audience members in the adjacent theater.

When police arrived, they found Holmes standing by his car in the parking lot. He was cooperative and did not resist arrest.

Twelve people died in the massacre; another 70 were injured.

The Aftermath

During the competency hearing, two court-appointed forensic psychiatrists declared Holmes as sane at the time of the shooting. While he was being evaluated, Holmes referred to the people that he wounded as "collateral damage," stressing that, at the time of the shooting, he was focused on how many people he could kill.

On July 16, the jury returned a guilty verdict on 12 counts of first-degree murder, 140 counts of attempted first-degree murder, and one count of possessing explosives.

Holmes was sentenced to 12 consecutive life sentences, with an additional 3,318 years added.

III

Elliot Rodger

SINCE THE AGE OF 17, ELLIOT OLIVER ROBERTSON Rodger had been obsessed with thoughts of taking revenge on everyone who had wronged him. The people who topped his list were women. The anger and resentment would finally be released on May 23, 2014, the day he terrorized a college town.

Wanting to Belong

Elliot Rodger was born July 24, 1991, in London, England. His parents, Peter and Li Chin Rodger, both worked in the movie industry. Peter was a filmmaker, and Li Chin was a research assistant.

The family moved to Los Angles, California, when Rodger was five. His parents did well in their new city, and Rodger enjoyed a somewhat privileged life. A major turning point occurred, however, when his parents divorced. Rodger was seven at the time and took it personally. He felt as though having divorced parents was just something that should not happen to him. He felt like he was being rejected.

He attended Crespi Carmelite High School, a private school. He transferred schools several times before graduating in 2009 from Independence Continuation High School. Teachers and students remember Rodger as being extremely shy and timid; he would rarely speak. As a result, he was an easy target for bullying.

Rodger wrote in his diary that he cried every day that he went to school. He felt that everyone was out to get him and had no one to turn to. Though his parents sent him to therapists since he was eight years old, no diagnosis was ever established. He was prescribed antipsychotic medication but refused to take them.

In high school, Rodger felt like a complete outsider. He never got involved in typical high school experiences like dating, partying, or going to dances. His lack of involvement with girls was particularly painful for him. His high school was full of girls who he would have loved to get to know, but none of them seemed interested in him, and he started to develop resentment toward them. He also felt anger toward the boys to whom the girls seemed to be drawn. He felt that they were pathetic losers. He would later state that, from the age of 17, he had obsessively fantasized about killing those who he felt had done him wrong, especially girls.

Online Confessions and Declarations

The online environment felt safe to Rodger. He spent a lot of time in a misogynous chatroom, which consisted of members who were involuntarily celibate. They would exchange hateful messages about women. He also opened a YouTube account where he would post videos discussing the anger he felt and describing how a plan to get back at those who rejected him.

Having never been in a relationship with a female, Rodger's first introduction to sex was through pornography. The subject of sex was a sore point for Rodger. It became even more so when he enrolled at the University of Santa Barbara and rented an apartment near Isla Vista, an unincorporated area near Santa Barbara.

With all the co-eds around him, his anger toward women increased as he realized that being in a college environment had not changed anything for him. From his distorted and narcissistic perspective, he saw himself as being superior to other males. He believed that he was the perfect partner for any woman. He saw himself as coming from money, being brilliant, and being the alpha male. He could not understand why women did not want to be with him. In his mind, he felt that they deserved to be punished. In one YouTube video, he said:

> "I'm 22 years old and I'm still a virgin. I've never even kissed a girl. I've been through college for two and a half years, more than that actually, and I'm still a virgin. It has been very torturous. College is the time when everyone experiences those things such as sex and fun and pleasure. Within those years, I've had to rot in loneliness. It's not fair. You girls have never been attracted to me. I don't know why you girls aren't attracted to me, but I will punish you all for it. It's an injustice, a crime, because…I don't know what you don't see in me. I'm the perfect guy, and yet you throw yourselves at these obnoxious men instead of me, the supreme gentleman."

Rodger dropped out of the university soon after enrolling and found himself spending a lot of time online or watching young couples from a distance. Jealousy and envy were the two emotions that dominated his life. He had an uncontrollable fixation on watching young couples, which only caused his rage to grow. That rage deepened his commitment to work on his plans for retribution.

Toward the end of April 2014, Rodger started writing his manifesto, titled, "My Twisted World," outlining his plan to carry out his revenge on the world. The following are some excerpts from his manifesto:

> "I am Elliot Rodger…Magnificent, glorious, supreme, eminent…Divine! I am the closest thing there is to a living god."

> "Humanity is a disgusting, depraved and evil species. It is my purpose to punish them all. On the day of Retribution, I will truly be a powerful god, punishing everyone I deem to be impure."

> "This is the story of my entire life. It is a dark story of sadness, anger, and hatred. It is a story of a war against cruel injustice…I didn't want things to turn out this way, but humanity forced my hand."

"Women should not have the right to choose who to mate and breed with. That decision should be made for them by rational men of intelligence. If women continue to have rights, they will only hinder the advancement of the human race by breeding with degenerate men and creating stupid, degenerate offspring."

"Women are like a plague. They don't deserve to have any rights. Women are vicious, evil, barbaric animals, and they need to be treated as such."

He also wrote that he wanted to:

"Quarantine women in concentration camps. At these camps, the vast majority of the female population will be deliberately starved to death. That would be an efficient and fitting way to kill them all off… I would have an enormous tower built just for myself…and gleefully watch them all die."

"In an ideal world, sexuality…must be outlawed. In a world without sex, humanity will be pure and civilized. Men will grow up healthily, without having to worry about such a barbaric act…In order to completely abolish sex, women themselves would have to be abolished. In order to carry this out, there must exist a new and powerful type of government, under the control of one divine ruler, such as myself."

"How could an inferior, ugly black boy be able to get a white girl and not me? I am beautiful, and I am half white myself. I am descended from British aristocracy. He is descended from slaves."

"On the day before the Day of Retribution, I will start the First Phase of my vengeance: Silently killing as many people as I can around Isla Vista by luring them into my apartment through some form of trickery."

"The Second Phase will take place on the Day of Retribution itself, just before the climactic massacre…My War on Women…I will attack the very girls who represent everything I hate in the female gender: The hottest sorority of UCSB."

On May 22nd, Rodger posted his last video online. The following is an excerpt from that video:

"Well, this is my last video, it all has to come to this. Tomorrow is the day of retribution, the day in which I will have my revenge against humanity, against all of you. For the last eight years of my life, ever since I hit puberty, I've been forced to endure an existence of loneliness, rejection and unfulfilled desires all because girls have never been attracted to me. Girls gave their affection, and sex and love to other men but never to me."

Carrying Out the Plan

Rodger had three roommates: Weihan Wang, Cheng Yuan Hong, and George Chen. Wang, aged 22, was a student at the University of Santa Barbara and was planning to move back in with his parents. Wang was getting frustrated with Rodger's unsocial manner and the way he played loud music late at night. Hong was from Taipei and was studying computer science at the university. Chen, aged 19, was interested in engineering and wanted to get a job with Lockheed Martin, an aerospace and defense company.

In his manifesto, Rodger indicated that he hated immigrants and minorities, especially when he saw them with girlfriends. He could not understand how women could go for a minority when they could have him. On May 23rd, Rodger waited alone in the apartment for his roommates to arrive. Using a machete and knife, he picked off each roommate as they arrived home.

Wang was the first to arrive, immediately heading to the room that he shared with Hong. Rodger followed and stabbed Wang repeatedly until he was dead. Soon afterward, Hong came home. Hong went to his room and screamed when he saw Wang's bloody body. Rodger approached Hong from behind and stabbed him to death as well. He piled Hong's body on top of Wang's and covered them both with a pile of dirty laundry.

Chen was the last to arrive. As he entered the apartment, he spotted Rodger. Rodger charged Chen, who tried to escape. He ran into the bathroom and tried to close the door, but he was too late. Rodger forced his way into the bathroom and stabbed him repeatedly. Chen's blood covered the tile floor. Rodger took his weapons, hopped into his BMW, and took off to his next target; the sorority house Alpha Phi, he had mentioned his manifesto.

Rodger aggressively knocked on the sorority's door; however, there was no answer. He assumed no one was home. Frustrated, Rodger was starting to walk back to his car when he spotted three students. Veronika Weiss, Katherine Cooper, and Bianca Dekock;

all members of Alpha Phi and were returning from the main campus. Rodger shot all three of them multiple times; only Dekock survived.

Rodger did not know that there had been people home at Alpha Phi. Rachel Glikes, who lived in the house, had heard Rodger's knocking but had not answered the door. When the knocking stopped, she heard multiple gunshots and a woman screaming. The house mother, Linda Gordon, also heard the gunshots. She gathered all the girls in the house and took them to a safe place.

At 9:27 p.m., the Santa Barbra County dispatch center received a call from someone who reported hearing gunshots. Police converged on the sorority house while Rodger drove off on Pardall Road. His murder spree had only just begun. As he drove, he passed a coffee shop. He briefly stopped in the middle of the road, fired a shot into the coffee shop's window, and took off.

The Isla Vista Deli Mart was a popular place for students and that evening was no different. A group of students standing on the street corner heard the gunshot that Rodger fired into the coffee shop down the road. They ran inside the deli as a precaution. One student named Christopher Michaels-Martinez stood in the doorway of the deli, trying to see what was happening outside. Rodger stopped his car in front of the Isla Vista Deli Mart and sprayed it with gunfire. Martinez was hit in the chest and died on the spot. Inside the deli, bullets and broken glass went flying as students dove for cover. Satisfied, Rodger took off in search of his next victim.

As he approached the corner of Embarcadero Del Norte and Madrid Road, Rodger spotted a man crossing the street. He hit the gas and plowed into the man, causing him to go flying into the air. Remarkably, the man, Jin Fu, received only minor injuries. Rodger continued driving. He knew the police would catch up with him soon. As he drove, he fired at anyone he saw and used his car to hit several other individuals.

Eventually, the police spotted him, and they were in hot pursuit. Rodger managed to create distance between himself and the squad cars behind him. Then he crashed into a parked car. When the police arrived at the crash scene, they converged on Rodger's crashed vehicle, with guns drawn.

It was too late. Rodger had beaten them to it. He had committed suicide by shooting himself in the head.

Rodger's rampage lasted only eight minutes. In those eight minutes, six people were killed, fourteen were wounded, and over 500 rounds were fired.

IV

Zachery Bowen

TWENTY-EIGHT-YEAR-OLD ZACHERY BOWEN SAT at the bar of the Omni Royal Hotel, in New Orleans. He finished his last drink and contemplated his life. He felt he failed in the way he handled things.

There were two failures among many that stood out. The first was, he had taken the life of his girlfriend. The second was, he felt no remorse for doing so. It was time. He walked toward the outside terrace and looked down below.

War and Coming Home

According to those who knew him, Bowen was just an ordinary guy who never drew attention to himself. That is until he joined the military. Bowen got married at the age of 18, and he and his wife had two children.

He decided to join the army so he could better support his young family. Bowen quickly rose in ranks, becoming a sergeant during his tours in Kosovo and Iraq. Around this time, those who served with him saw a change in his personality. He became increasingly unhappy and clearly just wanted to go home. Bowen eventually received a general discharge and returned home.

Bowen was bitter about his military experience and angry with himself. He felt he had failed as a soldier. Like many veterans, he had trouble adjusting to civilian life. He and his wife separated soon after his return. Bowen decided it was time to get back on his feet and got a job bartending.

The French Quarter is a place that is abundant in temptations, ways to numb painful feelings. Women, alcohol, and drugs are readily available. Bowen became increasingly interested in Addie Hall, who bartended with him at the same establishment. Hall shared his love for drinking, and they soon moved into an apartment in Crescent City together.

Bowen needed a lot of attention; he needed a woman to distract him from his loneliness. However, Bowen did not realize he had entered a toxic relationship that would spiral downward and lead to the destruction of both of them.

The Storm Within

In August 2005, Hurricane Katrina hit the gulf coast with fury. The citizens of Louisiana were hit particularly hard. Most people were able to evacuate their homes. Bowen and Hall decided to stay and wait out the storm in their apartment. Being stuck in their home was the perfect excuse to engage in heavy drinking and use cocaine. Because they spent most of their time intoxicated, they gave little regard to the seriousness of the situation. Hall even stood in front of her window and flashed her breasts at rescue workers as they worked to save others from their flooded homes.

Like many of the region's residents, Bowen and Hall endured the aftermath of the storm, including massive power outages and lack of clean water. To them, this was all just another excuse to continue partying. They kept up their drinking and drug use, which heightened the tension between the two. Hall had a bad temper when she drank, and she released her anger on Bowen.

When conditions in the Crescent City began to normalize, a new hurricane hit. That new hurricane was the relationship Bowen and Hall found themselves in. Unlike Hurricane Katrina, this hurricane would prove fatal for both of them.

Bowen's depression approached a new level. His relationship with Hall was making his time in the military seem a walk in the park. Hall continuously unleashed her anger on him. He became the target of her emotional and physical abuse. They were constantly going at each other.

How Do You Like Your Meat Cooked?

On the morning of October 5, Bowen woke up with a pounding headache. He walked into the bathroom and looked in the mirror. He saw the face of a man mired in darkness. He had failed as a husband and father, he had failed the military because he couldn't handle it, and now his new girlfriend was always angry with him. What had he done with his life? At that moment, he felt that Hall had pulled the rug out from under him, right when he needed someone to care about him; she constantly persecuted him.

Bowen left the bathroom and grabbed his belt. He walked down the hallway until he reached the other bathroom. Hall was in the bathtub. In one quick movement, Bowen put the belt around her neck and began choking her. The more she struggled, the tighter he pulled the belt. He kept tightening the belt until there was no longer any movement from her body.

Killing her had not satisfied his anger. His rage was still burning. He went to the garage and returned to the bathroom with an electric saw. He drained the tub water and proceeded to decapitate and dismember Hall's body. He grabbed her head and carried it to the kitchen, where he placed it in a pot on top of the stove. He then returned to the bathroom and retrieved her hands and feet. Bowen placed them in a second pot and then placed her arms and legs on a turkey basting tray. He sprinkled the body parts with seasoning and placed them in the oven, which he then turned on. As for her torso, he put that in a large plastic bag and stored it in the refrigerator.

Self-Inflicted Justice

The anger and delusional thinking that led Bowen to murder his girlfriend savagely were now focused squarely on himself. At first, he attempted to distract his self-loathing by binge drinking, taking drugs, and spending time in strip joints. However, the power of these distractions was short-lived. His demons reappeared in full force. Reaching for a pack of cigarettes, Bowen removed one and lit it. He then proceeded to press the lit cigarette against his arm. The burning sensation was his purgatory. He took the cigarette and burned himself again and again. Each burn represented one year of his life: a total of 28 burns.

Bowen grabbed some paper and a pen and wrote a suicide note. He explained what he had done to Hall and where her body parts could be found. He shared his feelings of failure as a husband, father, and boyfriend. When he was done, he drove to the Omni Royal Hotel and had his last drink. After the last sip, he calmly walked to the outside terrace and jumped, killing himself instantly.

V

Byron Smith

THE DATE WAS APRIL 21, 2013. A JURY IN THE Morrison County courthouse listened to a chilling tape recording that had captured the sounds of two teenagers being slain.

The city of Little Falls, Minnesota, is located in Morrison County. One of its residents, 65-year-old Bryon Smith, was the defendant on trial.

Setting the Trap

A military veteran, Smith was becoming increasingly frustrated as his home had been burglarized eight times in the last few years. On Thanksgiving Day, 2012, he decided he was going to put an end to it. He got in his truck, pulled out of his driveway, and parked further up the street. He wanted to create the impression that he was not at home.

He grabbed his .22 caliber pistol, a paperback book, a bottle of water, some energy bars, and proceeded to head to his basement. He positioned a chair toward the rear of the basement, between two large pieces of furniture. Perched in his chair, he had a clear view of the bottom of the stairs. Smith ate one of the energy bars, had some water, and waited.

As Smith was reading his book, he heard something that sounded like glass breaking.

Next, he heard footsteps coming down the stairs. He pointed his gun and waited until 17-year-old Nick Brady came into view. Smith pulled the trigger and shot Brady, who was standing halfway down the stairs. Brady fell down the stairs, his body landing on the basement floor. Smith got up from his chair and shot Brady a second time, as he lay there, helpless. Smith stood over him. Looking into his face, he told Brady, "You're dead." Smith pointed his gun at the dying Brady and pumped one more bullet into him.

When he was sure that Brady was dead, Smith grabbed the body by the legs and pulled until it came to rest on top of a tarp that he had spread out on the floor. Grabbing the edges of the tarp, Smith dragged Brady's body to his workshop, which occupied the corner of the basement. He would later explain that he moved Brady to avoid getting blood on the carpet that partially covered the basement floor. Once he got the body to the workshop area, he wrapped the tarp around it.

Smith returned to his chair and waited. He did not have to wait for long. Eleven minutes later, Smith heard more footsteps coming down the stairs. He heard a female voice softly calling Brady's name. Seconds later, Smith spotted 18-year-old Haile Kifer. Smith shot her several times. Her body tumbled down the stairs.

As she lay sprawled on the floor, Smith could see that she was still alive. Smith approached her and told her, "Oh, sorry about that." Kifer screamed, "Oh my God!" Smith shot her again and then told her, "You are dying." Smith called her a bitch as she lay moaning; the sound of her labored breaths filled the air.

Seeing that she was still alive, he pointed his gun under her chin and fired the fatal shot. Brady later told investigators that the shot under her chin was "a good clean, finishing shot." He also said that when he shot her for the last time, "She gave out the death twitch."

Justifying on Tape

Smith remained in the basement for hours. As he talked to himself, his tape recorder picked up every word. He referred to the teenagers he had just killed as "vermin." He talked about how his actions were a service to the community. According to Smith, if the police had arrested them, they would have just been released after a short sentence. Once free, they would have gotten involved with drugs and more serious crimes. Smith talked about how he no longer had to live in fear.

He was initially charged with second-degree murder; however, the charges were later changed to first-degree murder with premeditation and two counts of second-degree murder. It only took the jury three hours to find Byron Smith guilty. He was sentenced to life in prison without the possibility of parole.

Mr. Smith submitted an appeal in November 2018.

VI
David A. Burke

DECEMBER 7, 1987, INVESTIGATORS FROM THE National Transportation Safety Board were searching for the remnants of Pacific Southwest Airlines Flight 1771, which had crashed near Cayucos.

Cayucos is a beach town in San Luis Obispo County in California. The investigators were searching the hillside when they discovered the remains of a handgun containing six shell casing; a piece of a finger was attached to the gun's trigger guard. They also found an air sickness bag with a note scribbled on it: "Hi, Ray. I think it's sort of ironical that we end up like this. I asked for some leniency for my family. Remember? Well, I got none and you'll get none."

Analysis of the finger by the Federal Bureau of Investigation revealed it belonged to David A. Burke.

Out of Control

Burke was born in Britain on May 18, 1952, to Jamaican parents. They later immigrated to Rochester, New York. As an adult, Burke moved to Los Angeles and worked as a ticket agent for USAir. He was never married but did manage to get four women pregnant, resulting in seven children.

One of the women he got involved with was Jacqueline Camacho, who also worked as a ticket agent at USAir. He had a violent temper, which was well-known by those who knew him, including former girlfriends, neighbors, and law enforcement.

The Firing

While working for USAir, Burke was accused of stealing in-flight cocktail receipts totaling $69. The airline held a hearing on December 7, 1987, to discuss the allegations. Despite Burke's plea for leniency, his supervisor, Raymond Frank Thomson, decided to fire him. Thomson left the hearing hastily to attend a meeting, but not before leaving Burke with these final words: "Have a nice day."

Burke's violent temper was released with a vengeance due to this turn of events. When he got home, he grabbed Camacho and her six-year-old daughter and ordered them into his car at gunpoint. They drove for six hours. During the drive, Burke ranted about how USAir had treated him. When he calmed down, Burke allowed Camacho to return home.

The next day, Burke returned to the airport to buy a ticket. He knew that Thomson regularly flew between Los Angeles and San Francisco. Even more specifically, he knew that Thomson would be taking PSA Flight 1771 that day. He had decided to teach Thomson a lesson for his lack of leniency. Before boarding, Burke called Camacho on his cell phone. He got her voicemail and left the following message: "Jackie, this is David. I'm on my way to San Francisco, Flight 1771. I love you. I really wish I could say more, but I do love you."

A Tragic Mistake

Burke's employer, Pacific Southwest Airlines, had made a tragic mistake due to an oversight. They had not forced him to surrender his USAir credentials when he was fired. Their mistake allowed Burke to bypass security checkpoints and board the plane with a .44 Magnum revolver, which he had borrowed from a co-worker. Flight 1771 departed Los Angeles at 3:30 p.m.; the flight to San Francisco would take 72 minutes.

The Deadly Skies

Burke found his seat, reached for the airsickness bag in front of him, and wrote a note on it. Passengers were advised that they could unbuckle their seatbelts at 22,000 feet. Burke left his seat and walked to where Tomson was sitting. He gave the startled Thomson the airsickness bag and then made his way to the lavatory. He closed the door behind him and withdrew the gun that he had hidden under his clothing. He loaded it and stepped out of the lavatory. Passengers screamed as Burke made his way down the aisle toward the horrified Thomson. Burke shot him twice and then made his way to the cockpit.

The pilot, 44-year Greg Lindamood, was at the controls. His co-pilot, 48-year-old James Nunn, was radioing air traffic control to inform them he had heard shots outside the cabin. Right at that moment, Burke burst into the cabin. He shot Lindamood and Nunn once each. Lindamood was killed instantly, while Nunn was incapacitated. Though he desperately tried to maintain control of the plane, he did not have the strength.

Douglas Arthur was the chief pilot for PSA flights to Los Angeles. He was aboard the flight as a passenger and aware of the unfolding crisis. He made his way toward the cockpit to regain control of the plane. When he opened the cockpit door, Burke shot him as well.

Forty-three people lost their lives in the crash, which resulted in new federal laws being passed. The legislation requires airlines to seize credentials from all terminated airline and airport employees immediately. Additionally, it requires such employees to pass the same security measures as passengers.

VII

George Hennard

THOUGH KILLEEN HAS A POPULATION OF ONLY 141,000, the Texas city became infamous on October 16, 1991. On that date, it was the focus of what would become the fourth deadliest massacre by a single shooter in U.S. history, as 35-year-old George Hennard unleashed years of anger on a Luby's restaurant.

Anger at Sea

Hennard was born on October 15, 1956, in Sayre, Pennsylvania. His father was a surgeon, and his mother was a homemaker. Hennard was the oldest of the three children. The family later moved to White Sands, New Mexico, where his father worked at the missile range.

He graduated from Mayfield High School in 1974, after which he joined the Navy. He was honorably discharged after serving three years and quick to join the merchant marines. For Hennard, being at sea was a way to avoid people. He held grudges against people, especially toward women and minorities. Hennard's life took a turn when the merchant marines fired him in 1981. His employer had received notice that Hennard had been fined for using marijuana.

An Explosive Mix

Hennard was a time bomb waiting to explode. Those he worked with knew he had a volatile temper. He would frequently throw things and punch holes in the walls when he was angry. Hennard was also a loner. His former supervisor said that he never saw him socializing with anyone while working as a merchant marine. His neighbors often reported him yelling and screaming late and night. The police frequently received calls from him. He would make complaints about his neighbors or request that they investigate sounds he heard, which turned out to be imaginary. To add further to this explosive mix, Hennard harbored a hatred for minorities and gay people. He especially hated women, who he often referred to a "snakes."

After being released from the merchant marines, Hennard had nowhere to go and had moved back in with his mother in Bell County. Now, at thirty-five, he found himself alone in his mother's small house. His mother had divorced his father while Hennard was away at sea.

Like many parts of the country, Bell County had been hit hard when the economy dipped. His mother had to close the antique store she ran. Hennard had not held a job for almost ten years.

Hennard felt like a victim. He believed that society was responsible for the circumstances in which he found himself. On October 16th, Hennard decided to strike back with full force. He armed himself with a Glock 17 semi-automatic and a 9mm Ruger P89 pistol. He got in his blue 1987 pickup truck and took Highway 91 to Killeen.

The Luby's Massacre

Luby's was a popular place to eat for the locals; however, there was an exceptionally large crowd on this particular day because it was Boss's Day; many people were out with their bosses. Hennard pulled up to the restaurant just before 1:00 p.m. He placed his truck so that it was facing the restaurant's large main window and hit the accelerator. As his truck barreled through the window, broken glass went flying. Several people and tables were thrown in the air by the truck's impact.

The truck did not come to a standstill until it reached the center of the restaurant. Screams and crying filled the air as people took refuge under their tables. His first two victims were two customers who he had hit with his truck. Hennard stood over them as they lay wounded. Without any emotion, he shot them both in the head.

He made his way down the serving line of the restaurant and methodically shot each person who came into view, aiming for the head. Hennard repeatedly yelled: "This is what Bell County did to me. Was it worth it?"

He headed to the main dining area and continued shooting, reloading twice as he circled the room. One man dove through a nearby window to escape; a few others followed him. Another man threw a chair at another window, allowing customers to escape. Two customers hid, one inside a walk-in refrigerator and another inside an industrial dishwasher.

One by one, Hennard picked off the patrons until he came across an old woman. She was kneeling over her dead husband as though trying to protect him. Hennard shot her in the head. He moved on to the next table. A mother and her child were hiding underneath. Hennard told the mother to take her child and get out, which they did. Hennard continued shooting. Except for the sound of gunfire and Hennard's rants, there was an eerie silence as those who were still alive remained motionless. Some held hands, while others prayed.

Just across from the Luby's, a hotel was hosting a Department of Public Safety conference about automobile theft. Some of the officers in attendance heard Hennard's shots and rushed to the restaurant. When they arrived on the scene, the officers could smell gunpowder coming from inside. They entered the restaurant and took cover behind the fallen tables. One of the officers felt a hand grabbing at his leg. It was a wounded customer who begged the officer to rescue him. A few seconds later, the man succumbed to his injuries and died.

One of the officers, a sergeant, pointed his gun at Hennard, who was some distance away. The sergeant was waiting to get a clear shot when Hennard disappeared into the men's room. With his last remaining bullet, Hennard shot himself in the head.

With Hennard dead, the officers surveyed the gruesome scene surrounding them. Dead bodies were piled on top of each other, and the floor was covered with blood, broken glass, and bullet shells. Twenty-three people had been killed, and twenty-seven were injured.

VIII
James Edward Pough

June 18, 1990, has gone down in infamy for the people of Jacksonville, Florida. It was on this date that James Edward Pough went on a devastating murder spree.

Mother's Little Helper

Pough, born February 16, 1948, grew up in Jacksonville. He was the youngest of nine children. His father left the family when Pough was nine. Pough had a close relationship with his mother and tried to support her by helping around the house, despite having asthma.

Growing up was difficult for Pough. Though he did his best to be the 'man of the house,' he was not emotionally mature enough to take on that role. Between the ages of 17 and 18, he was arrested six times for various crimes, including vagrancy, attempted robbery, and assault. He eventually decided to get his life back on track and started working as a laborer, which would become his vocation for the rest of his life. The agency that located jobs for him ranked him as one of their top workers for his reliability.

He attended college but dropped out shortly after his freshman year.

Violent Behavior

A pivotal moment for Pough occurred in 1987 when his mother died. From that day forward, he was on a downward emotional spiral and became increasingly violent. Theresa, his wife at the time, alleged domestic violence and received an injunction preventing Pough from having contact with her. Court records showed two instances where he threatened her with a gun, holding it to her head. They separated shortly after.

Pough moved to Jacksonville's Northwest Quadrant, where he rented an apartment in an old duplex. He also found a girlfriend.

On May 8, 1971, a close friend of Pough's, David Lee Pender, dropped by while Pough and his girlfriend were relaxing at home. During an argument, Pender called Pough's girlfriend a derogatory name.

Pough's girlfriend carried a .38 caliber pistol in her purse for protection. When Pough heard what Pender had said to his girlfriend, he exploded in anger. He grabbed the gun from his girlfriend's purse and put three bullets into Pender. Pender died while being treated at a hospital and Pough spent the rest of his life haunted by the memory of what he had done to his friend.

Pough was arrested and charged with murder; however, the charges were later downgraded to manslaughter. He avoided going to trial by pleading guilty to the lesser offense. Pough received five years of probation without jail time. The court agreed to withhold the judgment of guilt if he completed the terms of his probation. Because of the deal, Pough did not have a criminal record.

Reprocessed

After the trial was over, Pough became even more reclusive. He was a loner who kept a predictable schedule of going to work and coming home. Without family or friends, he was rapidly losing reasons to live.

One day, he decided to trade in his old car for a 1988 Pontiac Grand Am. The General Motors Acceptance Corporation loan office financed the car. Pough experienced difficulty in making his car payments, which were higher than those for his old car. His Grand AM was repossessed in January 1990. Pough continued not to make his payments to the loan office, resulting in him receiving a bill for $6,394.

He felt angry and upset about receiving the bill, which he just ignored. After all, in his mind, they were filthy rich, and he had nothing! He received a second bill from the loan office two months later, which further fueled his anger. He felt like the world was against him. His father had abandoned him, his mother had died, his wife had left him, his best friend was dead, and the car that was so important to him had been repossessed. Now that damn loan company was coming after him for $6,394. That was his breaking point, but Pugh decided he was not going down alone!

The Shooting Spree

On June 17, around 12:50 a.m., Plough got his M1 Carbine rifle, wrapped it up in a blanket, and drove to a street corner a few blocks from his home. He was on a mission. He could not take his life anymore and wanted to die. He was going to take as many people with him as he could.

The street corner that he drove to was very familiar to him. It was a common scene for prostitution and drug deals. Louis Carl Bacon, a pimp, was standing at the corner. Pough pointed his rifle and shot Bacon twice in the chest. He left him lying dead on the sidewalk and drove a short distance further along the street.

It was then that Pough spotted Doretta Drake, a sex worker. She was talking to some other sex workers in a vacant lot. Bacon was Drake's pimp, and Drake had once taken Pough's money without giving him sex. Pough shot her once in the head and drove on.

Pough noticed two teenagers walking on the sidewalk. He pulled up alongside them, acting as though he was lost. He asked them for directions to the freeway. After they assisted him, Pough thanked the youths, pulled out his rifle, and shot them both. The two youths were lucky; they survived their wounds.

In the early morning of June 18, Pough drove passed a convenience store. He made a U-turn and pulled into its parking lot. He got out of his car and entered the store, rifle in hand. Stepping up to the counter, he pointed his rifle at the clerk and demanded money. The clerk cooperated with Pough and gave him all the money from the register. Pough's next stop would have special significance for him.

After fleeing the convenience store, Pough traveled to the cemetery where his mother was buried. He had visited her regularly in the past. He knew that this visit would be his last; he wanted to speak to her one more time. When he was done, he called his supervisor and told him he was not going to be able to make it to work that day. It was time to make his final stop.

Pay Back at the Loan Office

The General Motors Acceptance Corporation loan office was located at 7870 Bay Meadows Way. Pough pulled into the parking lot and got out of the car. He had come prepared. He had an M1 Carbine, a .38 caliber revolver, loaded magazines, and extra ammunition on him. The sight of Pough entering the building caused instant panic in the loan office. Two customers at the counter, Julia Burgess and David Hendrix, tried to run, while office workers dove under their desks.

Screams rang out as Pough fired at Burgess and Hendrix. Hendrix was injured but would survive; Burgess was not as fortunate. Pough then made his way into the office area. He fired at the person hiding beneath each desk he passed. Dave Woods, Cynthia Perry, and Barbara Holland died, while Phyllis Griggs survived her injuries.

Employees working in the back office heard the shooting and tried to escape through a back entrance. While some of the employees managed to get away, others were not so lucky. Among those who did not escape were Janice David, Sharon Hall, Lee Simonton, Ron Echevarria, Nancy Dill, Denise Highfill, and Jewell Belote. Pough had accomplished what he had set out to do, but one final act remained. Pointing his .38 caliber revolver at his head, he pulled the trigger.

During the two-minute massacre at the loan office, Pough had fired over 28 rounds from his M1 Carbine, killing seven people and wounding six.

IX

Howard Unruh

It was the late evening of September 5, 1949, and 28-year-old Howard Barton Unruh was sitting in the movie theater. The double-feature playing was *The Lady Gambles*, and *I Cheated the Law*.

This was the third showing of this double feature that he had viewed since his arrival at the theater earlier that day. He had originally gone to the movie theater to meet up with another man, whom he was seeing. The movie theater on Market Street was a popular pick-up spot in the gay community. Unruh had arrived late to the theater, and his date had left by the time he had arrived. Instead of going home, he had decided to stay for the movie.

Though his eyes were directed toward the movie screen, his attention was on the thoughts that paraded through his head. He was mulling over all the ways his neighbors had persecuted him and how he could get back at them.

Coming Home

Unruh was born January 21, 1921, in East Camden, New Jersey. His parents, Samuel Shipley Unruh and Freda E. Vollmer, separated while Unruh and his little brother were very young. His mother raised the boys on her own.

Unruh drove a tank for the 342nd Armored Field Artillery in World War II. During the Battle of the Bulge, he became known for his bravery and his habit of taking meticulous notes. He kept a record of the German soldiers that were killed, describing the condition of their corpses in detail.

Unruh's military service ended in 1945 with an honorable discharge; however, his return to civilian life was accompanied by changes in his personality. Unruh had a hard time holding a job. He worked in the printing industry for a while. However, he quit after less than a year. At one point, Unruh pursued a professional career by enrolling at Temple University. He had decided to pursue a degree in pharmacy; however, again he quit quickly, this time after just two months.

He gave up looking for work and moved in with his mother. Unruh became reclusive, spending most of his time in his room. It was heavily decorated with memorabilia from his days in the military. His collection of medals and firearms covered the walls. He set up a target range in the basement.

Paranoia in the Neighborhood

Unruh's relationships with his neighbors were strained. He developed paranoid thoughts, believing his neighbors were out to get him. Just as he had done in the military, Unruh kept a detailed journal of all the ways his neighbors supposedly wronged him. He felt that the neighborhood tailor, Tom Zegrino, had repeatedly short-changed him. Zegrino's wife, Helga, had complained that Unruh played his music too loudly. He was upset with another neighbor for throwing trash on his property.

Unruh was also upset with thirty-three-year-old Clark Hoover, the neighborhood barber. He accused Hoover of dumping dirt in a drainage ditch, which resulted in Unruh's cellar flooding. The neighborhood cobbler, twenty-seven-year-old John Pilarchik, was another target of Unruh's discontent. Unruh was mad with him for burying his trash too close to his property line. Another source of anger was the neighborhood teen who had tapped into Unruh's electrical line to get power for his Christmas tree business. More than anything, Unruh was upset with the local teenagers who called him "queer" and "mama's boy." This especially bothered him because he was worried that they might have seen him hanging around the movie theater on Market Street.

Unruh had a girlfriend once, but the relationship lasted only a year. They met while he was serving in the military. He never had sex with his girlfriend, and he broke it off when she expressed the desire to get married. Since the break-up, Unruh had been with numerous men. Despite dropping out of Temple University, he had kept his room in a nearby lodging house and remained there another year after quitting school. During that period, Unruh spent his time with different men throughout the day.

Unruh stayed in the movie theater until 2:30 a.m. and then left to go back home. He had built a gated fence around his mother's home as a result of the paranoia he had regarding his neighbors. When he arrived home around 3:00 a.m., he saw that the gate to his fence had been stolen. The theft of his gate was the proverbial straw that broke the camel's back. Most people who knew Unruh would describe him as being meek and someone who would not hurt a fly. They did not know that Unruh was a man about to explode.

Unruh had trouble sleeping due to his paranoia and building anger. He woke up around 8:00 a.m., ready to carry out his plan to strike back. He got dressed in a suit, white shirt, tie, and army boots. Armed with his .38 caliber, Unruh made his way to the back door, which was in the kitchen.

He encountered his mother, who became alarmed when she saw the gun. He threatened her with a wrench, she ran out of the house and headed for a neighbor's. Unruh exited the back door, made his way across the yard, and headed for the 3200 Block on River Road.

Walk of Death

As he made his way down River Road, Unruh saw a bakery truck parked on the side of the street. Seconds later, he saw the driver walking toward his truck. Unruh aimed and fired. Fortunately for the driver, Unruh missed him. He ran to his truck and sped off.

Unruh's first stop was at Pilarchik's shop. As he entered the store, he shot Pilarchik in the chest. Pilarchik collapsed to the floor. When he saw that Pilarchik was still alive, Unruh shot him in the head, continuing his "walk of death."

Hoover was in his barbershop, cutting the hair of a six-year-old boy as his mother patiently waited. Suddenly, there was gunfire and a scream. Unruh had shot the boy once in the head; he shot Hoover twice. Both died. The mother grabbed her dead son and ran out of the store. Unruh allowed her to escape. She and her dead son were picked up by a passing motorist.

As he continued his walk down River Road, Unruh passed a tavern and fired a shot through the window. He did not bother going inside as Frank Engel, the owner, was not on his list. Instead, Unruh proceeded toward the pharmacy owned by Maurice Cohen.

Forty-five-year-old James Hutton was exiting the pharmacy just as Unruh was about to enter. Unruh dropped him with one shot and stepped over his dead body into the pharmacy. Cohen and his wife, Rose, had witnessed Hutton being shot and had run for the stairs that lead to their apartment above the pharmacy. Unruh casually followed them.

When he reached the upstairs apartment, he forced his way inside. As he walked in, he heard a soft noise coming from the closet. He fired three shots into the closet door and then opened it. It was Rose. He shot her one more time in the face and then went searching for her husband. Unruh heard footsteps on the roof and headed for the fire escape. As he did, he passed a room and saw Maurice's mother inside. She was on the phone, talking to the police. He shot her repeatedly, then headed for the roof. Before reaching the roof, Unruh saw Cohen on the roof. Cohen tried to run. Unruh shot him in the back. Cohen fell off the edge of the roof and landed on the pavement below.

Unruh exited the pharmacy and continued his walk. He fired at passing motorists, killing four of them. He killed an additional motorist who had stopped by Hutton's body. Unruh walked to the tailor shop: he was after Tom Zegrino. Upon entering the shop, he saw that Tom was not there. Instead, he found Zegrino's wife, Helga. Crying, she dropped to her knees and begged for her life. He shot her in the head, killing her instantly. As he left the store, he noticed a movement of the curtains in the store next door. Unruh shot into the window, killing two-week-old Thomas Hamilton. The curtains were dangling inside his crib, and he was playing with them. By the time he exited the store, the entire business district had caught on to the shooting spree. Business owners offered pedestrians refuge as they locked themselves inside their stores.

Unruh now headed to his apartment. On his way, he passed the apartment next door, where thirty-six Madeline Harrie and her 16-year-old son, Armand, lived. He fired at them, and both were wounded. Fortunately for them, Unruh had run out of ammunition. Then he heard police sirens headed in his direction.

Fifty police officers surrounded Unruh's apartment. In 1949, mass shootings were unheard of, so the police did not have the training to handle the situation. After they sent a hail of bullets into Unruh's apartment, he eventually gave up. In 20 minutes, Unruh had taken the lives of 13 people. Four others had been severely wounded.

Criminally Insane

During his interrogation, Unruh accepted full responsibility for what he had done and offered the details of his crime in a clinical and detached manner. A psychiatrist evaluated him and found him to be suffering from paranoid schizophrenia.

October 20, 1949, a judge of Camden County ruled that Unruh was not competent to stand trial. Instead, he was sent to

Trenton Psychiatric Hospital, where he was placed in the unit for the criminally insane. He was sentenced to 60 years.

He died in 2009.

X
Angela Simpson

IN THE EARLY MORNING OF AUGUST 5, 2009, THE Peoria Fire Department received a call that smoke had been spotted coming from the Covenant of Grace Church.

Peoria is a city in Maricopa County, just west of Phoenix, Arizona. It is a quiet and unassuming city; however, in 2009, it was the starting point of an investigation that would uncover, according to detectives, one of the most hideous murder cases in the history of the Phoenix Police.

To Kill a Snitch

Thirty-three-year-old Angela Simpson was smoking a cigarette on August 2, outside her West Phoenix apartment. Forty-six-year-old Terry Neely, riding his motorized wheelchair, approached her. Neely lived at an assisted living center nearby. Simpson barely knew Neely but had held brief conversations with him in the past.

During one conversation, Neely had boasted about being a police informant. He further indicated that he had snitched on someone whom Simpson knew; someone that she felt was "a righteous person." There were two types of people Simpson believed deserved to be killed: Police informants and child molesters. A black woman herself, Simpson viewed Neely as "white trash."

Simpson used her feminine charms and invited Neely over to her apartment for sex and drugs. Neely was excited by the offer and followed Simpson as she led him to apartment #201. Once they were in her apartment, Simpson stood before Neely and slowly approached him. Neely was unable to take his eyes off her as he anticipated all the pleasure he was about to experience.

When she was directly in front of them, Simpson gave him a hard slap across the face. Neely yelled out in pain as he was knocked to the side in his wheelchair. She moved behind the wheelchair and pushed Neely until he was in front of a wall-length mirror. Simpson wanted him to witness everything she was about to do to him.

She grabbed a tire iron and repeatedly beat him over the head. Blood flowed from his head as he began to lose consciousness. Simpson spotted some pliers on a table, grabbed them, and demanded Neely open his mouth. The blow he received left him dazed and withering in pain. She grabbed his head and forced it back. With her other hand, she pulled out his teeth, one by one, as Neely screamed in pain. His head was soaked in blood and more dripped from his toothless mouth. Barely alive, he slipped from his wheelchair to the floor.

On the same table as the pliers were a hammer and a three-inch nail. Simpson grabbed the hammer and nail and drove the nail into Neely's skull. He moaned in pain. Blood from his mouth wounds drained down his throat, causing him to cough. Simpson grabbed an electric cord, wrapped it around his neck, and choked him. She finished him off by slitting his throat with a knife and stabbing his body repeatedly.

Simpson stood over Neely's dead body; the carpet around him soaked in blood. She was faced with the problem of what to do with the body. She knew she is not able to move it alone, so she got an electric saw and dismembered the body. She put Neely's torso in a garbage bag, placed it in her car, and drove to the Covenant of Grace Church. Upon arriving at the church, she placed the bag in a trashcan in the parking lot. Simpson poured lighter fluid on the bag and ignited it with a lit match. Neely's torso became engulfed in flames as Simpson sped away from the scene.

Investigation and Conviction

Firefighters discovered Neely's torso when they were putting out the fire. Later, police found Neely's electric wheelchair outside a West Phoenix apartment. Detectives could not establish a connection between the torso and the wheelchair, nor did they have any leads. They received a big break when Simpson was arrested for an armed robbery that she committed in the same month that she had murdered Neely.

Police went to her apartment to search for more evidence. Upon entering, they discovered that it was cleared out. All that remained was a strong bleach smell. The police were able to find blood evidence that matched the DNA of the torso. Simpson freely confessed to murdering Neely. She was sentenced to life in prison with an additional 14 years for abandoning a body.

No Regrets

Simpson has been very open about her feelings regarding her crimes since her conviction. When asked why she murdered Neely, she replied, "I don't want my children or the people I consider family to be in a place where there are snitches…I believe informants and child molesters should be killed."

She also told interviewers that she does not feel at all guilty for killing Neely, stating, "I'm a little upset that I won't be able to, you know, kill more snitches, but I have no remorse about killing him [Neely]."

When asked why she had him face a mirror during his murder, she stated, "He needed to see what he deserved."

When asked about how she felt knowing she would be spending the rest of her life in prison, she replied, "You know I've got a lot of family in prison…I'm okay with that. I've got many sisters in prison. I can't wait to see 'em. It's really not that much of a punishment to be sentenced to spend my life with my family."

Simpson explained that she has a history of mental illness going back to when she was just ten years old but insisted that she does not want or expect sympathy. She also said she believes she deserved the death penalty but is happy with her sentence.

When asked if she would ever kill again, she replied without hesitation, "If the opportunity arises, I hope so."

XI

Thomas Michael Lane

THOMAS MICHAEL LANE III ENTERED THE courtroom wearing a dress shirt and long pants. His court date would give the families of the three students he had killed an opportunity to present their victim impact statements to him.

Eighteen-year-old Lane sat down and started to take off his shirt so he could display the t-shirt he wore underneath. In large letters, Lane had written the word, *Killer*. He smirked when family members exposed their raw pain and grief as they read their statements.

After the judge handed down his sentence, Lane faced the families and stated, "This hand that pulled the trigger that killed your sons now masturbates to the memory. Fuck all of you!" He then gave the middle finger to the families.

A Broken Home

Born September 19th, 1994, Lane's home life was extremely dysfunctional. His father, Thomas Lane II, had served time four years in prison for charges that included attempted murder and felonious assault. He terrorized his family and would frequently beat Lane's mother. The stress, fear, and isolation that Lane III experienced while being raised in such a horrific environment would contribute to a deadly outcome.

Problems at School

Because of his upbringing, Lane never had the opportunity to develop trust, confidence, or a sense of self. He did poorly in school, was withdrawn, and rarely spoke to others. He was also the subject of bullying.

Lane's grandparents adopted him and attempted to provide him with a nurturing home. His grades improved, and neighbors had the impression he was a pleasant and friendly young man. However, Lane had still had a lot of rage within him. He was arrested twice for participating in an attack on his uncle with his cousin and for physically assaulting another boy.

He was originally enrolled at Chardon High School, but they referred him to Lake County Educational Service Center, a school that specialized in working with students that have academic or behavioral needs. If he completed the school's program, Lane would be able to graduate with his classmates from Chardon. His grades improved dramatically; however, he kept to himself and was still bullied.

Cafeteria Massacre

On February 27th, 2012, seventeen-year-old Lane walked into the cafeteria at Chardon High School. He was waiting for the bus that would take him to Lake County Educational Service Center. It was 7:30 a.m., and the cafeteria was full of students eating breakfast. Eleven hundred students attended Chardon and around one hundred of them were in the cafeteria that morning.

Among the students eating breakfast were sixteen-year-old Daniel Parmertor, seventeen-year-old Russell King, sixteen-year-old Nate Mueller, and seventeen-year-old Nick Walczak. The four boys were sitting at the same table as they joked around and ate their breakfast. Russell was dating Lane's ex-girlfriend.

Without any warning, Lane pulled out a Ruger MK III Target .22 caliber semi-automatic handgun and began firing. Panic and chaos broke out as students dropped their food trays and ran for safety. Some of the students ran for the exits while others dove under their tables for cover.

Lane walked over toward the table where the four boys were sitting and aimed. The first bullet missed its target and grazed the ear of a sixth-grade student, Nate Mueller, who was walking nearby. Mueller ran toward the exit and escaped. Until he was grazed by the bullet, he had not even realized a shooting was occurring. Lane shot again, this time accurately. Parmertor died instantly. King was seriously wounded, and a boy, Demetrius Hewlin, sitting at another table.

Walczak ran toward the exit as Lane fired at him repeatedly. He shot Walczak in the neck, arms, back, and one bullet entered his cheek. Despite his multiple wounds, Walczak ran down the hall and escaped. He collapsed outside the classroom of the math teacher, Joe Ricci. Upon hearing the gunshots, Ricci had locked down his classroom. The well-being of the students was Ricci's top priority. He slowly opened his classroom door to check for any students left outside who needed help. He saw Walczak and dragged him to the safety of the classroom, where he administered first aid. After shooting at Walczak, Lane ran for the exit to escape. On the way, he came across eighteen-year-old Joy Rickers. He shot her, injuring her, and continued with his escape.

Coach Frank Hall had heard the shooting and ran for the cafeteria, entering at the opposite end to where Lane had exited. Beyond the traumatized students, Hall could just make out Lane running out of the building. Hall took off after him, disregarding his own safety.

While the shooting was in progress, one of the students had called 9-11 using their cell phone. Thirty-three police officers descended on the high school, along with emergency crews from four fire departments. They located Lane near his parked car, where they arrested him without incident.

Charges, Competency, and Sentencing

March 1st, 2012, Lane was charged with three counts of aggravated murder, two counts of aggravated murder, and one count of felonious assault. He did not enter a plea and was arraigned on March 6th. He had three defense attorneys representing him. By the judge's decision, Lane would not be tried until he was evaluated for competency. They scheduled another hearing to determine if he would be tried as an adult or juvenile.

According to Ohio law, "a child may be found competent only if able to grasp the seriousness of the charges, if able to understand the court proceedings, if able to aid in the defense, and if able to understand potential consequences. A child with a mental illness, or an intellectual or developmental disability may not be found competent."

The court held Lane's competency hearing on May 2nd, 2012. A psychiatrist, Dr. Phillip Resnick, testified that Lane was mentally ill. Although he diagnosed Lane with psychosis, he determined that Lane was able to understand the crimes with which he was charged. It was determined that Lane was competent to stand trial.

March 19th, 2013, Lane was tried as an adult. He pleaded guilty and was sentenced to three life sentences in prison.

XII

James Huberty

JULY 17, 1984, JAMES OLIVER HUBERTY CALLED THE San Ysidro Health Center, located in California. He wanted to schedule an appointment to see someone. The representative who answered Huberty's call asked him if he would like to discuss his concerns. Huberty declined. He said he just wanted to schedule an appointment with a therapist.

As part of standard procedure, the representative asked Huberty five questions that are used for screening callers to assess their level of risk to themselves or others. Based on his responses and his calm tone of voice, the representative advised him that a therapist would be calling him back to schedule an appointment.

Huberty did not get a callback. It is possible that if he had, the worst mass shooting in the history of the United States might have been prevented.

Background

Huberty was born on October 11, 1942, in Canton, Ohio. His parents, Earl V. and Icle Huberty, moved the family from Canton to Pennsylvania when James was around eight years old. His father had bought a farm located in Amish country. Icle was unhappy living in Amish country and left her family to pursue missionary work on an Indian reservation. Huberty's father would later get remarried to a schoolteacher who had children of her own. James never got along with his stepmother and resented his parents' divorce.

In 1962, James started attending Malone College, where he would meet his future wife, Etna Markland. They married in 1965 and moved to the city of Massillon, where they had two children. Huberty worked as a welder, a big departure from his previous job in a mortuary, where he had worked as an embalmer. He had left that job after a few years. His boss would later say that his embalming skills were good, but he did not like being around the public.

Huberty's neighbors and co-workers knew him as someone who never smiled, was easily angered, and often talked about his desire to shoot people. He was known for his temper, his love of guns, and his violent streak. Whenever Huberty felt disrespected by his neighbors, Huberty would take out his anger by shooting from his balcony. His wife also had issues with her temper. She was once arrested for threatening another woman with a gun.

The Survivalist

Huberty was a survivalist and pre-occupied with his thoughts of government intrusion, Soviet aggression, and international banking. He believed that America was headed for a breakdown. He felt that government regulations were causing the demise of businesses, that international bankers were bankrupting the country, and that nuclear war with the Russians was inevitable. He stockpiled his home with weapons and perishable foods.

In 1971, the Huberty's home burned down. They bought a new home with their insurance settlement and had enough money left over to purchase an apartment adjacent to their property. They used the apartment as an investment property. For the first time in his life, James felt like he was somebody and he could take care of his family. However, his financial security would not last.

In October of 1983, Huberty was let go from Union Metal Inc., where he worked as a welder. This only confirmed to him that his fears were correct. Huberty believed that government regulations were the reason he had lost his job; the government was trying to keep him down and prevent him from taking care of his family. His paranoia toward the government led him to request permission from Mexico to establish residency there.

Huberty was granted this permission and moved his family to Tijuana. Living in Tijuana allowed him to escape the U.S. government; however, he was unhappy with his living conditions and the lack of opportunities for work. Consequently, Huberty then moved his family to San Ysidro, California. San Ysidro was a small community near San Diego, which allowed him greater opportunities to find work. He also liked that it was close to the border, just in case they needed to leave the United States.

Life in San Ysidro

Huberty rented a small apartment, one block away from a McDonald's restaurant. The apartment was sparsely furnished as the family had left most of their belongings in storage back in Ohio. Huberty had brought some things along though: his stockpile of weapons and perishable foods. There were so many weapons in the tiny apartment that he was always in arm's reach of a weapon should he ever need it.

Huberty got a job working security at a condominium; however, he was eventually dismissed. His supervisor was concerned about his lack of professionalism and his questionable decision-making. His supervisor later stated that Huberty's coworkers would sometimes laugh at him for the way he handled himself on the job, which they said was "over the top."

Huberty sat in his room alone as his family watched television in the living room. Being fired was the final blow. He saw no future for his life and did not see how he would be able to care for his family. Huberty looked at the guns and rifles scattered around him. In a few days, he would get back at a society that he believed was out to get him.

Judgment Day

On the morning of July 18th, Huberty drove to a courthouse in San Diego to take care of some traffic tickets he had received. He brought his family with him so they could visit the San Diego Zoo afterward. Before going to the zoo, they stopped at a McDonald's restaurant to eat.

After spending the day at the zoo, Hubert and his family drove back to their apartment in San Ysidro. His wife was tired and went to their bedroom to take a nap; however, Huberty had plans of his own. He changed into his fatigues, along with some accessories: a leather shoulder bag filled with ammunition, and a fourteen-shot clip that he fastened to his belt. For the final touch, he grabbed his 9-mm Uzi semi-automatic, a Winchester pump-action 12-gauge shotgun, and a 9 mm Browning HP.

Huberty's wife saw he was about to leave and asked him where he was going. He kissed her goodbye, something that he had rarely done in the past, and told her that he was going out to hunt humans. Etna did not take him seriously as he always had a dark sense of humor. Huberty got into his old, beat-up Mercury Marquis and drove to the McDonald's restaurant on San Ysidro Boulevard, just a block away.

This McDonalds was mainly patronized by Mexicans and Mexican-Americans. Huberty blamed Mexican immigrants for taking jobs away from Americans, including his. He entered the restaurant at 3:40 p.m. and yelled, "Everyone get down!" He immediately began showering the restaurant with bullets from his Uzi. Chaos broke out as the unsuspecting crowd and employees sought refuge.

Some of Huberty's shots sprayed outside and struck three small boys who were riding their bicycles to the restaurant. Two of the boys were killed instantly. The third boy played dead. Inside the restaurant, customers dropped to the floor, hid under their tables, or ran for the exits as broken glass and bullets went flying.

Seventeen-year-old Wendy Flanagan was working at the restaurant. When the first gunshot rang out, she thought it was a firecracker. A co-worker grabbed her hand and pulled her behind the counter. Lying on the floor, Wendy felt her co-worker's grip release from her hand. She turned around and saw that her coworker was dead.

Between the sounds of bullets firing, there were intermittent periods of almost silence, punctuated by the soft sounds of people moaning and praying. A few babies were crying. These periods of silence were broken by the sound of gunfire as Huberty systematically executed each person he encountered as he made his way around the restaurant. One customer, who had been hit, was playing dead. She opened her eyes briefly to evaluate what was happening, but Huberty caught her in the act, cursed at her, and then shot her several times.

Some customers were able to sneak behind the counter to where Wendy was lying. She guided them to a storage area in the back of the restaurant, and they silently waited. They later heard someone trying to get in. Whoever was outside the door was banging on it, hard. Suddenly the banging stopped, and Wendy heard a thud. She opened the door and saw her co-worker Alberto Leos. He had been shot several times and was bleeding profusely. They dragged his body into the storage area and used their shoelaces as tourniquets. Alberto bit down on a piece of cloth to prevent Huberty from hearing him, as he struggled with the pain.

Meanwhile, outside, police surrounded the restaurant. They could see bodies scattered around the entrance. The restaurant's tinted windows were cracked from the gunfire, preventing the SWAT team from gaining a visual of what was happening inside. Eventually, a sniper from the SWAT team was able to get a clear shot and eliminated Huberty with a bullet to the heart. The massacre lasted over an hour and claimed the lives of 21 people. 20 were wounded. The victims' ages were 8 months to 74 years old. Huberty had shot 257 rounds of ammunition in what was the nation's most deadly shooting at the time.

After the Nightmare

There were so many bodies that authorities used the San Ysidro Civic Center to hold wakes. The local funeral homes were not able to accommodate all the families of the victims. Back to back funeral masses were held at the Mount Carmel Church.

McDonald's corporate headquarters began work on renovating the bullet-ridden restaurant only two days after the shooting. However, their efforts were in vain, as community leaders successfully argued that the location should never open again. McDonald's donated 1 million dollars to a fund that was set up for the survivors, and founder Ray Kroc's wife donated an additional $100,000. A memorial park was built in place of the restaurant, containing 21 marble pillars, one for each victim.

In 1986, Huberty's wife filed a lawsuit against McDonald's restaurant and her husband's former employer. In the $7.5 million complaint, she argued that the combination of eating chicken McNuggets, which contain MSG, and fumes he had inhaled while working there, had caused her husband to commit the massacre. Needless to say, her suit was thrown out.

Finding that they had been ill-equipped to handle the shooting, the San Diego Police Department scaled up their training and equipment. One officer confided that Huberty's .38 caliber revolver had outmatched his service revolver.

Conclusion

YOU HAVE JUST READ ABOUT TWELVE PEOPLE who terrorized others because they could no longer deal with their anger and upset.

They committed ghastly murders that most of us could not even imagine doing. You may have noticed some familiar patterns while reading their stories. Most, if not all of them, felt isolated and saw themselves as victims of a society that they perceived was out to get them.

They felt like failures in life and blamed these failures on everyone but themselves. Each person in this book reached a tipping point, a point from which they cut loose and lashed out with a vengeance at those they blamed for their painful lives.

Until we learn to reach out to those in need, we will continue to risk the wrath of these killers.

List of Twelve Volume 3

12 Terrifying True Crime Murder Cases

Introduction

IN VOLUME 3 OF THE TRUE CRIME SERIES, YOU WILL be treated to 12 new profiles of some pretty savage killers. The murderers in this volume took their killing to a whole new level. They ate their victims!

Volume 3 is about killer cannibals.

Most of us could never take the life of another unless it was a matter of life or death, self-defense, or protecting a loved one. If most people are incapable of taking the life of another human being, what kind of mind is willing to kill and eat another person? As you read Volume 3, you may be surprised to find out who these people are. In this volume, you will read about:

- Austin Harrouff: Florida teenager who went berserk and ate a stranger's face.
- Stanley Dean Baker: Hitchhiking hippie who carried human finger bones to chew on.
- Albert Fentress: New York teacher who killed a neighborhood boy and ate his body parts.
- Omaima Aree Nelson: Egyptian beauty who made a rib dinner out of her American husband.
- Antron Singleton: Inspiring rapper who killed and ate a Los Angeles woman.
- Marc Sappington: Kansas City youth who became known as the Kansas City Vampire.
- Alex Kinyua: Brain-eating university student.
- Otty Sanchez: Texas woman whose voices led her to cannibalize her baby.
- Tyree Lincoln Smith: Connecticut man who consumed the body of the man who woke him.
- Joseph Oberhansley: Deeply troubled man who cooked then ate his girlfriend after she dumped him.
- Gregory Scott Hale: Depraved Tennessee man who wanted to be the next Night Stalker and took it to the next level.

- Joe Metheny: Four-hundred-and-fifty-pound cannibal who served his victim's flesh to the customers of his barbecue stand.

As with every volume in the True Crime Series, you will read detailed profiles that include each murderer's background, details of their crime, and their legal aftermath.

Get ready to enter the world of those who committed the greatest taboo: the cannibal killers.

I
Austin Harrouff

IT WAS A HOT AUGUST DAY IN JUPITER, FLORIDA, and the Harrouff family was having lunch at Duffy's Sports bar. They were joined by their nineteen-year-old son, Austin, who was visiting his parents for the weekend.

Austin was growing impatient and becoming restless as he waited for his order to arrive. His parents, Wade and Mina Harrouff, tried to calm him down. Something that Wade said to Austin only compounded his restlessness. Austin could no longer contain himself and abruptly got up from the table and stormed out of the restaurant. He was walking back to his parent's home, which was three miles away, when he felt a familiar feeling overcome him.

The fear that he experienced would later spark a bizarre and horrific crime that would receive national attention.

Frat Boy Behaves Strangely

Born December 21st, 1996, Harrouff was a native of Jupiter. Besides his parents, he had a sister named Haley. Harrouff was well-liked by all those who knew him. He was seen to be nice, helpful, and polite. An active child, he loved sports. In high school, he was on the wrestling team and played football. His muscular body and good looks made him stand out in a crowd. He later attended Florida State University, where he majored in exercise science. He also belonged to the fraternity Alpha Delta Phi.

In the months leading to that fateful August day, those who knew Harrouff noted significant changes in his behavior. It started off with him telling his parents that their house was haunted. He became so upset by this that he moved his bed into the garage, which was to become his new room.

In particular, he was fearful of a demon he referred to as Daniel. He also told his mother that he had superhuman powers and was sent to Earth to help others. One day, Mina was cooking and had prepared a bowl containing cooking oil and cheese. She had stepped out of the kitchen to get something. When she returned, she caught her son drinking cooking oil, straight from the bottle, and eating the mixture from the bowel.

The Demon Made Him Do It

It was because of his strange behaviors that his mother became alarmed when he stormed out of Duffy's on August 16th, 2016. She called the Jupiter police department and his fraternity to assist her in finding him. When she spoke with the police, she informed them he was not a danger to himself or others. Her statements were not without merit. Harrouff was not violent, did not take drugs, nor had he ever been charged with a crime. Still, she had a bad feeling about the situation. Unfortunately, her concerns would come true.

Under the sweltering heat of the day, Harrouff walked home from Duffy's. He lived on Southeast Kokomo Lane, almost three miles away. With every step he took, the fear within him grew stronger. Soon, he was in fear for his life. He felt the presence of Daniel looming over him.

As he walked, he began stripping off clothes until he was semi-naked. He did not remove his clothes because of heat as much as it was to escape a strange feeling he was experiencing, a feeling he could not explain. Harrouff would later say in an interview, "I just needed to find someone to help me to figure out where I am…I don't even remember what I said to myself. I just remember being afraid, scared." That interview would be with Dr. Phil McGraw but would never air.

John Stevens and Michelle Mishcon were a married couple who lived close to the Harrouff house. Stevens was 59 and worked as a landscaper. Mishcon was 53, and a housewife. They would routinely bring their portable television to the driveway, where they would watch it. It gave them the opportunity to enjoy the open air and chat with people passing by. On this day, Mishcon sat in her folding chair, watching her show. The garage door was open, and Stevens was inside the house. He was finishing up on a project and was planning to join his wife outside.

The glass of lemonade she was drinking was almost empty, so Mishcon got up from her folding chair and went inside for a refill. She entered the house through the garage; it was at this point when Harrouff found himself in front of their home. He did not know Stevens or Mishcon. He did not know why he was there or how he got there. All Harrouff knew was that he was feeling afraid and not feeling like himself. He walked up the driveway and made his way into the garage.

Inside the garage, he saw tools hanging neatly on the wall. He also saw cans of paint and bottles of different liquids. He grabbed a bottle, removed the lid, and drank from it. He felt a burning sensation in his throat. It was at that point Mishcon stepped back into the garage. She let out a scream as she saw the near-naked Harrouff standing in their garage. Harrouff was just as surprised to see her. Her screams aggravated him. He hit her repeatedly with his fist until she succumbed to his beatings and lay motionless on the garage floor. Harrouff saw a machete on the wall and grabbed it. He swung it at her multiple times, leaving deep cuts in her lifeless body.

Turning around, Harrouff saw Stevens in the doorway that led to the garage. Stevens saw his wife's body on the floor of the garage. Before he could even react, Harrouff ran at him. Stevens ran in the house, but it was no use; Harrouff was much faster than him. He beat Stevens and then stabbed him repeatedly with a pocket knife he carried.

Jeff Fisher, who lived in the neighborhood, heard Mishcon's screams and headed over to investigate. Before he could see Mishcon's body, Harrouff charged him. Fisher ran away, but Harrouff stabbed him three times. Fisher was able to escape and run home, where he called 911.

A Grisly Feast

Deputies from the Martin County Sheriff's department arrived at the house of Stevens and Mishcon. They found Mishcon's blood-soaked body in the garage. As bad as that was, they were greeted by a sight even more horrific when they entered the home. In the living room, they discovered Harrouff on top of Stevens, who was barely alive. Harrouff was chewing on the side of Stevens's face as he made animal-like sounds.

The deputies ordered Harrouff to get off Stevens, but he refused. They used a stun gun on him, but it didn't affect him. Harrouff did not get off Stevens till police dogs were released on him. It took three deputies to restrain him after due to the incredible strength he exhibited. As the three deputies secured him, another deputy checked on Stevens. It was too late; he was dead. Harrouff yelled at the deputies, "Fucking kill me, fucking kill me! Shoot me now! I deserve it!"

Harrouff was arrested and taken to the sheriff's station, where detectives interviewed him. While not denying anything, he was not able to explain why he committed the crime. As the interview progressed, Harrouff claimed his throat was burning. He was taken to the emergency room, where he was examined; his esophagus was burned from the chemical he drank in Stevens garage. He had pieces of human flesh and hair stuck between his teeth.

The Dr. Phil Interview

Harrouff was hospitalized at St. Mary's Hospital for treatment of his chemical burn. He slipped into a coma for 11 days, preventing him from being formally arrested. As they waited for Harrouff to awaken from his coma, the sheriff's department requested a blood sample. It was tested for hallucinogenic drugs, due to his bizarre behavior and great strength displayed while being arrested, they were sure he must have taken something. To their surprise, his blood test came back clean.

While he was still in the hospital, and after waking from the coma, Harrouff was interviewed by the Dr. Phil Show via Skype. The following are some excerpts from the interview:

When Phil McGraw asked him how he felt about what he had done, he responded, "I felt terrible. And I really, really don't have words to explain how I feel. It's like, it's like a nightmare."

McGraw asked him what his thoughts were about what happened. Harrouff replied, "It's the hardest thing I've ever gone through. I never imaged this would ever happen. And I'm deeply sorry to the family affected. I hope something like this never happens again. I didn't ever want to consciously do something like this. I never planned it. I didn't want to do it. And, like, I don't know what to say."

When asked what he would like to say to the victim's family, he replied, "I'm sorry for their loss. And I hope that you can all find it in your hearts to forgive me. And I'm so sorry, and I never wanted this to happen."

Harrouff was very emotional during the interview, often breaking down in tears. Those who knew him could not conceive of him committing a crime, let alone one so horrendous.

Self-Identity Investigation

Another puzzling piece of his past was a letter he wrote himself January 6th, 2014:

> *The way I see myself may or may not be different from the way others see me. I view myself as happy, shy, nice, positive, and I never give up. I view myself as happy because usually I have view things to feel sad or depressed about. One of the main things I dislike about myself is that I am shy. I want to be confident and assertive. I am not*

that shy around close friends because after I get to know someone, I'll start to open up more toward them. I also see myself as nice because I will go out of my way to help people.

Harrouff was formally arrested upon being discharged from the hospital and charged with two counts of first-degree murder and one count of attempted murder. At his arraignment, he pled not guilty, and the prosecution agreed not to seek the death penalty.

His trial is set to begin on June 17th, 2019.

On another legal note: The Dr. Phil interview was released to a local news station after a legal request was made under Florida's public information law. Harrouff's defense lawyer argued that the release of the interview would be prejudicial against his client; however, a circuit judge from Martin County ruled in favor of the news station.

II

Stanley Dean Baker

IT WAS JULY 13, 1970, AND HIGHWAY PATROL officer Randy Newton was on patrol in Big Sur, California. He was driving the Pacific Coast Highway when he received a call from dispatch that two men, who were involved in a traffic accident, had fled the scene. He was advised the two men had taken off on foot in his area.

Newton exited the main highway and took a dirt road where the two men were last seen. After a brief drive, he spotted two men in the distance. One of the men was approximately six feet in height, shoulder-length blond hair, a beard, and powerfully built. He was wearing an Army fatigues jacket and jeans. His companion had long dark hair, a beard, wearing a green army field jacket, jeans, and cowboy boots.

Newton pulled up to the men and exited his patrol car. The blond-haired man was 22-year-old Stanley Dean Baker, and his companion was 20-year-old Harry Alan Stroup (in some stories, the name has also been spelled as Harry Allen Stroup). Both men were upfront with Newton and admitted to being involved in the traffic accident. This routine stop would take a turn when Barker made a bizarre statement, "'I have a problem. I am a cannibal." At first, Newton did not take him seriously, until Baker pulled two human finger bones out of his pocket.

Hitchhiking Across America

Both Barker and Stroup were born in Sheridan, Wyoming. Baker, once an altar boy and a boy scout, while growing up in Sheridan, never got in trouble with the law. Stroup did socialize with drug users but never actually got into trouble with the law. Baker did start to get involved with drugs after he was dismissed from the Navy for misconduct. He got involved with a satanic cult known as Four Pi Movement, a cult rumored to have committed murders for ritualistic purposes.

In June of 1970, Baker and Stroup left Sheridan to hitchhike toward the western coast. The following events are based on Baker's account of the murder:

When they reached Montana, the two men split up. Baker wanted to continue going while Stroup wanted to find a place to rest. They decided that Baker would explore the area and come back to meet up with Stroup later. As Baker walked along the side of the freeway, he could see dark clouds gather on the horizon of the Montana sky. Having lived all his life in Sheridan, thumbing his way across the county gave him a sense of freedom.

In his pocket, Baker had a piece of paper on which he had written down the ingredients to make LSD. He and Stroup had taken LSD before reaching Montana and were hoping to manufacture it when they reached California. The hippie culture was growing there, and they knew they could make easy money. He also had a copy of the Satanic Bible. He was recruited to the Four Pi Movement while living in Wyoming and was a follower of the cult's leader, Grand Chingon.

As he walked along the side of the freeway, a 1969 Opel Kadett slowed down for him. The driver of the car was 22-year-old James Schlosser. Schlosser was a social worker at the Musselshell County

Welfare Office. He was a large man over six feet tall and 200 pounds, with big frame glasses, and style of dress that gave him a nerdish appearance; a sharp contrast to Baker's scruffy and unkempt look. Schlosser believed in helping others and offered Baker a ride.

Carnage At The National Park

As the two men took off, Schlosser mentioned to Baker that he was headed for Yellow Stone Park. An avid fisherman, he wanted to camp out for the night and get some fishing in. Baker asked if he could join him, and Schlosser agreed.

The two men found a camping site close to the river. It was getting late, so their plans for fishing would have to wait until the next day. That night, both men slept on the ground. Because of the warm temperature, they did not pitch a tent. The warm temperature, the thunder and lightning of a distant storm, the seclusion, and LSD he had taken earlier, woke Baker's dark side.

Baker reached for the .22 caliber pistol he kept on him. While Schlosser was sleeping, Baker shot him in the head. A savage fury took over Baker. For him, having killed Schlosser was not enough. He reached for his hunting knife. Without putting much thought to it, Baker stabbed Schlosser twenty-five times. After Schlosser was dead, Baker cut a large t-shape in his chest, spread his chest wide open and using the knife, he broke Schlosser's rib cage open and pulled out his heart. Baker proceeded to consume Schlosser's heart under the stars.

After consuming the heart, Baker's face was stained with blood, and his beard was matted with it. He stared at Schlosser's body. Grabbing his knife again, he dismembered Schlosser's corpse. He removed the head, arms, and legs, which he cut off at the knees. Baker tossed the torso in the river and discarded the other body parts throughout the park. When he finished disposing of the body parts, he washed off in the river. Though he tried to get the blood out of his clothing, the stains remained. Returning to the campsite, he drove off in Schlosser's car. As Baker drove away from the park, he saw Stroup hitchhiking. He picked him up, and they headed for California.

On Saturday, July 11th, a man was fishing on the Yellowstone River. He felt his line snag on something heavy. He managed to reel in his line, where he made a shocking discovery. He had reeled in a human torso. The fisherman drove to the nearest telephone and called the ranger station at the park's entrance. Deputy Bigelow answered the call and was advised of the situation.

Deputies arrived at the site where the torso was discovered. They waded into the river and pulled the waterlogged torso out onto the banks. They searched the river and surrounding area but were unable to locate any other body parts. They also faced another challenge. The Yellowstone River crosses several states, so they could not determine where the torso was originally dumped. While investigators continued to search for evidence, the torso was sent to the morgue.

Connecting The Dots

On Monday, the Livingston Sheriff's department received a teletype regarding a missing person's report. The subject of that report was James Schlosser. The description provided in the report closely resembled that of the torso. Results of a DNA test confirmed the sheriffs' suspicion.

Baker and Stroup reached Monterey County, California. Driving Schlosser's Opel Kadett, they were approaching Big Sur. Baker did not realize it, but he was driving on the wrong side of the road. He was caught off guard when he saw a pick-up truck coming right at him. The collision between the two vehicles resulted in the Opel taking on major damage; however, the pick-up truck received only a dented bumper.

The driver of the pick-up truck approached Baker and Stroup to make sure they were okay and to exchange information. Baker told the other driver he did not have a driver's license. The other driver asked the two men to get into his truck, to which they agreed. They drove to the nearest phone to call the police so an accident report could be completed.

The driver and his two passengers drove to a service station in the town of Lucia. As soon as the driver parked his truck, Baker and Stroup bailed out of the car and took off running toward a wooded area. The driver called the California Highway Patrol to report the incident; it was Officer Newton who answered the call.

Officer Newton caught-up with Baker and Stroup, who admitted to causing the traffic accident. Given the lack of any identification, Newton arrested both men after reinforcements arrived. While driving back to the police station, Baker and Stroup freely conversed with the officer, sharing that they were from Sheridan, Wyoming, and had hitchhiked across the country.

The two men were brought to the station and interrogated. When asked about the finger bones, Baker told investigators he kept them to chew on, as he had developed a desire for human flesh since the age of 17. He also revealed he had received electric shock therapy for a nervous disorder.

While they were being questioned, detectives hit pay dirt. They received information that the Opel Kadett Baker and Stroup had been in was registered to Schlosser, whose torso had been found in Yellowstone River. The detectives split up Baker and Stroup to interrogate them separately. While interviewing Baker, Detectives were surprised by how open he was, boasting about his involvement in Schlosser's murder, claiming sole responsibility for it.

Pride In Murder

Baker and Stroup were extradited back to Montana, where they were arraigned on July 27th. They were detained at the Park County jail until August 4th. That was when Baker was sent to Warm Springs State Hospital for a psychiatric evaluation. Unlike Baker, who was an open book about the murder, Stroup remained silent and proclaimed his innocence. Prosecutors were getting frustrated because they had no evidence directly linking him to the murder.

Baker was found competent to stand trial and tried separately from Stroup. During his trial, Baker conducted himself in a manner that was anything but typical for a defendant. He continued to brag that he was the mastermind of the murder, and Stroup played no part in it. He made claims that he was Jesus and used mind control to make rock legend Jimi Hendrix overdose on drugs. At one point, he told the presiding judge to, "Go fuck yourself." When the judge reprimanded him, he responded, "What are you going to do? I am already sentenced to life in prison."

October 20th, the jury found Baker guilty of first-degree murder and sentenced him to life in prison, with an additional ten days for his remarks to the judge.

Thanksgiving Day was when Stroup was found guilty of manslaughter, as there was enough evidence to demonstrate he was somehow involved. The jury was convinced that Stroup had played a role in Schlosser's death. They did not believe that Baker could not have butchered Schlosser alone, given Schlosser's size. Park rangers also testified they saw Baker, Stroup, and Schlosser in the Opel Kadett when they arrived at Yellowstone Park. Further, the vehicle's odometer indicated that Baker did not make any extra trips to pick-up Stroup.

Baker also confessed to an unsolved murder in San Francisco. On April 20, 1970, the body of 40-year-old Robert Salem was discovered. Salem was stabbed 27 times, including a deep cut in his neck where the killer had attempted to decapitate him. Additionally, his left ear was missing.

The killer had used Salem's blood to write the words "Zodiac" and "Satan Saves" on the walls of the home. Investigators were unable to locate proof to tie Baker to his murder.

Baker was out by Christmas 1986, after 16 years. He died in 1994 from cancer. Because of the short time spent in prison, Montana changed their minimum of years served, and prisoners could not apply for parole before 30 years of their sentence were served.

Stroup was released after two years. He was convicted of selling meth in April 2007 and released in 2015. He served more time for a drug conviction than being an accomplice in the murder and cannibalism of Schlosser. He is still alive at 69 years old.

III

Albert Fentress

ALBERT FENTRESS WOKE UP FROM HIS DAZE AND found himself sitting at his desk. He had been experiencing dissociative states since he was young, especially during times of stress. Whenever he came out from his daze, it was like waking up from a dream. As in the past, he had no memory of what happened before waking up. He did not know why he was sitting at his desk.

He was about to get up when he noticed a sheet of paper with writing on it. As he read it, he became distressed. The paper offered a detailed account of a teenager being tortured and murdered; it was written in the style of a screenplay. Horrified by what he read, he crumpled up the paper and burned it. Fentress may have thought he'd destroyed the paper; however, its writing would become all too real in the days ahead.

The Eccentric Teacher

Fentress was born in 1941 (exact date unknown) in Brooklyn, New York. His father was a tough disciplinarian and believed in using physical punishment against him and his two younger siblings. A bright child, Fentress graduated top ten of his high school class. Ambitious, he was goal-oriented and wanted to become successful. With interest in history and teaching, he attended college to pursue his dream. He earned two masters' degrees; one in history and the other in education.

Upon graduation, Fentress got a job as a history teacher at Poughkeepsie Middle school. Fentress became a rising star in the classroom and earned the reputation of being among the top teachers in the New York area.

As his father was to him, Fentress had a strict disposition with his students. He also had some unconventional approaches to teaching, which school administrators tolerated due to his popularity as a teacher. An example of this was the time his class was studying World War II. Fentress came to school dressed up in a Nazi military uniform.

Fentress lived a reclusive existence. He never married, had no romantic interests, and had only a few friends. For him, the world of material goods was his source of emotional attachment. Also, the impression others had of him was very important to him. Though he was a middle school teacher, he drove a Cadillac, wore a Rolex, and kept his home in meticulous condition. He also took great pride in his stamp collection.

His emotional connection to his property was exemplified when he stated the lowest point in his life was when he had to leave his Cadillac at a shop for repairs. There was one other incident that rivaled the distress he felt over his Cadillac; when his stamp collection was stolen. That incident triggered a tragic episode for the Poughkeepsie community and received national attention.

Because of his strict disciplinary behavior as a teacher, along with his personal quirks, some of his students who lived in his neighborhood would tease him, and even sneak on to his property and commit acts of vandalism. The ultimate provocation was committed in August 1979. Fentress arrived home to find his house had been broken into and his prized stamp collection stolen.

Fentress was livid over the incident; he felt disrespected and violated. In his mind, he was convinced he knew who was responsible; it was 18-year-old Paul Masters. Fentress contacted the police and demanded they arrest him. The police advised him they could not arrest Masters without evidence he had committed the crime. Fentress grew more upset.

How could he be persecuted without receiving justice for what that teenage delinquent had done to him? He began to feel himself slipping into a daze. In his mind, he needed to strike back; he needed to protect his castle! He applied for a gun permit, after which he came up with a plan.

Best Laid Plans Taken To The Extreme

Though he had developed a plan to deal with Masters, it would be his depraved dark side that would take over. It would be that part of him, the part of him he kept concealed that would take charge in carrying out his revenge.

Fentress frequently watched out for any teenagers that may try to re-commit acts of vandalism or theft. On August 20th, Fentress spotted Masters climbing over his fence and landing on his property. Fentress decided he would use a psychological approach with Masters. Instead of threatening him or calling the police, who were of little help, he would entice Masters into a trap.

The student panicked when Fentress stepped into the backyard, as he did not think he was home. Fentress reassured Masters he was not angry and wanted to mend any hard feelings between them. He asked him if he would like to join him inside for a beer and to talk. Masters was visibly relieved and accepted his offer.

As they walked into the home, Fentress asked Masters about how he was doing in school. As they made small talk, Fentress told him he needed to go in the basement. He asked Masters if he would go with him as he could use help. Masters politely agreed.

As they walked down the basement stairs, Fentress replayed the scene from the movie *Deliverance* in his mind. Upon reaching the bottom, Fentress pulled out his gun and pointed it at Masters. Masters turned white as a sheet, as the blood drained from his face. Fentress ordered him to walk to a pole that stood in the center of the basement. Masters was shaking and crying, begging him not to shoot. Ignoring his pleas, Fentress ordered him to take off his pants and to face the pole. He had Masters extend his arms along each side of the pole, where he bound his hands.

Masters was weeping as he heard Fentress unzip his pants. The pain was excruciating as Fentress violated him from behind. He screamed as Fentress moved in and out of him. Suddenly, he heard Fentress curse, and he stepped back. Fentress had gone into his daze and was unable to perform. Out of anger, he shot Masters twice in the head.

Fentress sat down to rest. The dark desire within him remained unappeased. He needed to do more. When he had caught his breath, he untied Masters and proceeded to castrate him. He took the boy's genitals upstairs and into the kitchen. Fentress cooked the testicles and then had them for dinner. After he finished eating, he returned to the basement. He dragged Masters' body upstairs into his bedroom, where Fentress collapsed on his bed and fell asleep.

Upon waking up, Fentress saw the student's body on his bedroom floor. He realized what he had done and called a friend, explaining what happened. The friend called the police, who arrested Fentress without incident.

Releasing A Killer?

Due to the findings of his psychological evaluation, the judge determined that Fentress was not guilty due to insanity and sent him to a mental institution in New York. He was diagnosed as having narcissistic personality disorder, dissociative fugues, and obsessive-compulsive disorder.

It was in the mental institution he would receive, for the first time in his life, medication for his mental illness. After spending over ten years in the psychiatric ward, psychiatrists and lawyers argued he should be released because he had become a model patient.

A judge ordered a trial to determine if Fentress should be released, to avoid a lengthy appeal process. The psychiatrist who evaluated Fentress for the trail stated, "If he couldn't handle kids slashing his screens and burning his lawn, then how could he possibly handle the likely public reaction to his release, after he'd been demonized in the media as 'New York's own Hannibal Lector?'"

The jury returned a verdict that Fentress should be released. At 57-years-old, Fentress was released into a half-way house. After public outcry, including from Governor George E. Pataki, the state's Supreme Court ruled to overturn the jury's verdict. Fentress was to remain confined in the mental institution.

Multiple appeals have been launched by Fentress. His last appeal in 2014, at 72-years-old, was denied.

IV

Omaima Aree Nelson

TO AUTHORITIES, TWENTY-ONE-YEAR-OLD Omaima Aree Nelson did not fit the profile of a killer. The Egyptian-born beauty had dark black hair, olive skin, big brown eyes, with a slim build. She was accused of committing the most gruesome murder in the history of Orange County, California. Nor could they believe their ears when she made the comment: "Nothing tastes as good as the man I married. It's the sauce that does it."

Seeking A Better Life

Omaima was born in 1968 (exact date unknown) and moved to the United States in the early 1980s. She always wanted to live the California lifestyle. For her, it would be a chance to leave behind her life in Egypt, where she had been victimized. As part of her culture, she experienced genital mutilation and had been sexually assaulted twice by different men.

In October of 1991, Omaima went to a bar and met 56-year-old William Nelson, who was playing pool. Nelson was a large man, standing 6'4" and over 220 pounds. He was attracted to the exotic beauty, as were other men. Within days, the two got married. The newlyweds moved to Costa Mesa, a city within Orange County, where they rented an apartment.

A Relationship Gone Bad

Omaima soon found her marriage unraveling as William began to reveal his abusive side. He assaulted her multiple times. Whenever he forced himself on her or acted violently, she relived her memories from her past. He also expected her to participate in bondage and other fetishes. He would have her tie him up and perform sexual acts on him. Not only was she receiving abuse, but she was also expected to administer it to her husband. Before meeting William, Omaima had a boyfriend named Robert Hannson, who was from Huntington Beach. They had separated in 1990. He had also wanted her to engage in bondage with him.

In 1991, the tension between Omaima and William reached a climax on Thanksgiving Day. William assaulted her again. Additionally, he threw her kitten out the window of his red Corvette while driving. Upon entering their apartment, Omaima was hysterical when she stopped herself. She did not want to take any chances of William unleashing his temper on her again. To please him, she acted as though she was sexually interested in him. She seductively asked him if she could tie him up, which he quickly agreed to.

Dressed To Kill

She tied up her husband, making sure his arms and legs were secured to the bed frame. Seeing him restrained before her did not do much for her sense of safety. She experienced the same feelings of terror she'd experienced when she had been subjected to genital mutilation. She did not know it, but she was experiencing post-traumatic stress disorder. Like many abused women, she feared her husband but felt trapped. It was at that moment she snapped.

Reaching for the clothing iron, she bludgeoned him with it, causing him to yell out in pain. She hit him several more times with it, yelling and cursing at him the whole time. As her rage continued to grow, she grabbed a pair of scissors and stabbed him with them repeatedly. She had to stop her assault to catch her breath.

Staring at William's bloodied and lifeless body, she realized she had a problem. What was she going to do with him now? She went to the kitchen, grabbed a large knife and a clever, and returned to the bedroom. With a sense of determination, she proceeded to decapitate and dismember her husband's body. For her small size, it was an excruciating task, but she managed to do it.

She felt like she was outside herself as she became further detached from reality. Calmly, she took his head, placed it in a pot, and turned on the stove. When his head was cooked, she placed it in the refrigerator.

Omaima placed his hands in another pot and cooked them in oil to burn away his fingerprints. She used the garbage disposal to eliminate any remaining body parts that would fit, including his genitals, after she'd castrated him. Throughout the night, her neighbors heard her garbage disposal running. Unbeknownst to her neighbors, her garbage disposal was being fed an ongoing supply of body parts from her Thanksgiving turkey and her husband. She placed additional body parts in a suitcase and the freezer.

There was a part of his body that she had special plans for, his ribs. While his ribs baked in the oven, she went to her bedroom to change. She put on a red hat, red shoes, and red lipstick. When she heard the oven timer go off, she took out his ribs and ate her grisly dinner. She would later state they were just like the ribs prepared in a restaurant.

There were still body parts that were too large for her to handle. On December 2nd, she called a friend of hers and offered to pay him to eliminate the rest of her husband. Her friend agreed to help her; however, he notified the police instead. The police arrested her at home on the same day.

An Excuse To Kill?

On February 21st, Omaima appeared in Orange County Superior Court. She was charged with first-degree murder and pleaded innocent. She was also charged with assault on Hannson when she'd held him at gunpoint.

During the trial, her attorney testified she was psychotic at the time of the murder. He stated that her husband's abuse had triggered her extreme behavior.

The jury deliberated for six days and found her guilty of second-degree murder. She is serving 28 years to life at the Central California Women's Facility in Chowchilla, California.

In 2011, she was denied parole for a second time.

V

Antron Singleton

ALISA ALLEN LOOKED THROUGH THE WINDOW of her East Los Angeles apartment and witnessed something shocking. She saw a black man running naked in the street. His face, chest, and stomach were covered in blood. As he ran, he was looking up to the sky. She called the police.

When she hung up the phone, Allen ran to her friend's apartment. 21-year-old Tynisha Ysais had been spending time with Antron Singleton, the man she'd seen running in the street. When Allen entered Ysais' apartment, she let out a blood-curdling scream upon seeing what had happened to her friend.

Big Dreams

Antron Singleton was born on September 15th, 1976, in Fort Worth, Texas. However, he grew up in East Dallas. From the time he was a child, Singleton revealed his creative ability. By age seven, he started to write poetry and became inspired to become a rap artist. By age fifteen, he started to perform his music to the public any time the opportunity presented itself.

He started performing under the name G-Spade but would later change it to the Big Lurch. His new stage name was inspired by the 1960's television comedy, the Addams Family. The show depicted a ghoulish family, where the character of Lurch was the family's butler. Just as with Lurch, Singleton was of formidable size, measuring 6 feet 6 inches tall.

Singleton moved to California as he felt it held greater promise for making it in the music business. Through the years, Singleton achieved some musical success by performing on his own and as a member of a group. He worked with other rappers such as Luni Coleone, Mac Dre, RBL Posse, and the Oakland, California rap group known as the Cosmic Slop Shop. The Cosmic Slop Shop's 1998 album, Da Family, yielded the song *Sinful,* which became a minor hit. However, the group was not tight, and they broke up shortly after the release of Da Family.

Singleton kept trying, but he was getting discouraged. Establishing himself as an artist was more difficult than he had thought. His dreams of becoming a success became more elusive with each year that passed. In 2000, Singleton was driving home from his 24th birthday celebration when a drunken driver crashed into him. His injuries included a broken neck. During his stay in the hospital, he was heavily medicated for pain. The pain that he experienced would stay with him long after being discharged from the hospital. It also would play a role in a gruesome murder.

The Devil's Drug

Thomas Moore and his 21-year-old girlfriend, Tynisha Ysais, lived in South East Los Angeles. Their apartment on 108 Street and Figueroa were in a distressed area of the city. It was located next to the Harbor Freeway, two liquor stores, and a cheap hotel. On April 19th, 2002, Moore and Singleton got together to smoke PCP. Singleton used PCP because it relieved him from his lingering pain. Singleton knew Moore from the music business and was visiting the area to record an album. Ysais was not at the apartment, as she and her two children were visiting a friend.

On April 20th, in the afternoon, Singleton experienced a powerful pain. The painkilling comfort from the night before was rapidly fading. Looking around his shabby apartment, he realized he was out of drugs. A horrific feeling rushed over him. It was a feeling that surfaced from the darkest part of him; a darkness that could no longer be contained. Every pain and disappointment he'd ever had was presenting itself in full force. Singleton drove back to Moore's apartment to get more PCP from him.

Ysais was alone in the apartment. Her two children were in school and Moore was out. When she heard a knock on the door, she opened it just enough to see who it was. It was Singleton with a crazed look in his eyes. She immediately felt a chill rush through her as she knew this man was not all right. Singleton plowed his way into the apartment, knocking her down.

When she started screaming, Singleton beat her until she was quiet; the sounds of her screaming only intensified the fear he felt. He searched the apartment for the PCP but could not find any. The feeling of desperation, fear, and anger overwhelmed him. He grabbed a large kitchen knife from the kitchen and plunged into Ysais, causing her to release a chilling scream before she grew quiet. He stabbed her repeatedly in the chest.

At some point, while stabbing her, he realized it was not enough to satisfy his urge to destroy. Using the knife, he sliced open her chest cavity, grabbed her right lung, and began to feast on it. When he finished his morbid feast, he stripped off his clothes and ran out of the apartment.

Ysais' friend and neighbor, Alisa Allen, saw Singleton running down the street and called the police. The police arrived and arrested Singleton, who growled at them like an animal. Allen rushed to Ysais' apartment to make sure she was alright. It was then she was confronted with the most horrific sight that would haunt her for the rest of her life.

When the coroner examined her body, he found that she had multiple stab wounds, her neck and jaw were broken, and a fractured eye socket. Her chest had been ripped open, and she was missing her right lung. A three-inch knife blade had broken off near her left shoulder. When Singleton was examined, blood and pieces of human flesh were found inside his stomach. The blood and flesh were a match for his victim.

Unusual Representation

Singleton's trial was arraigned on June 13th, in Compton Superior Court. Upon hearing the evidence, Superior Court Judge Jack W. Morgan ruled that Singleton was sane at the time of the murder and would stand trial. His defense attorney was Milton Grimes, the owner of Singleton's record label, Black Market Records.

During his trial, his defense attorney argued that he had been under the influence of PCP at the time of the killing. A psychiatrist testified that Singleton suffered mental impairment due to his drug habit.

In less than one hour, the jury reached a guilty verdict. He was convicted of first-degree murder, torture, and aggravated mayhem.

Singleton is serving a life without the chance of parole. The judge added a second consecutive life sentence. He is serving his time at the California State Prison in Lancaster and has spent more time in solitary confinement than out of it.

VI

Mark Sappington

MARY WHITE CALLED OUT HER SON'S NAME BUT heard no reply. She and her son, Marc Sappington, lived together in a home located in Northeast Kansas City. They lived in an impoverished neighborhood that was crime-ridden. It occurred to her that perhaps he had gone to the basement.

White was walking down the basement stairs when she came to a freezing halt. She noticed drops of blood on the stairs. As she looked up, she screamed. The basement walls were splattered with blood. Rushing out of the basement, she called police.

White did everything that a mother could do; however, she was to discover that she had lost her son forever. It was not that her son had become another crime statistic. What she would find out is that her son was the Kansas City Vampire.

What's A Mother To Do?

Marc Sappington was born February 9th, 1978, and grew up in Kansas City, on the north side. His was a world of poverty. His mother was devoted to the church and held the same expectations for her son. His mother had a good reason for instilling her son with religious observance, as violence and crime were part of their neighborhood reality; many children fell victim to gang violence or joined them.

Sappington was liked by all those who knew him; he was intelligent and charismatic, and people naturally gravitated toward him. Unfortunately, for Sappington, the reality of his world was more persuasive than his mother's guidance. On March 16th, 2001, an event occurred that would be the starting point of his descent into an evil darkness.

Hanging With The Wrong Crowd

While walking around his neighborhood, Sappington met another boy his age, Armando Gaitan. Gaitan was everything that Sappington was not. Gaitan was a gangster wannabe, who lived by the code of the street. For some strange reason, Sappington liked him. Gaitan took Sappington to his clubhouse, where he showed him a black AK assault rifle. He told Sappington that to earn respect, "people needed to fear you." He invited Sappington to join him in testing out his new "toy."

The two boys were walking down a street when Gaitan told him he needed to make a stop. Gaitan walked into Phase One Auto Sales and confronted its owner, David Mashak. Gaitan bought a car from Phase One, but it was impounded. Gaitan demanded Mashak get his car out from the impound lot. Mashak blew off Gaitan for making such a ridiculous request.

Gaitan stormed out of the store, and Mashak resumed eating his lunch with one of his employees, Johnny Sublett. As they were eating, Sappington entered the shop with the rifle. Sublett ran for cover by escaping to the garage. He heard the gunshots from his hiding spot. When they stopped and he felt that it was safe, Sublett went back to the office. Mashak was lying on the floor, barely alive. Sublett called 911. When he hung the phone, he looked at the front door of the shop. It was open, and a crowd of people had gathered. The crowd knew what had happened. They were used to it.

That Sappington shot someone would be inconceivable to those who knew him. If those who loved him knew the truth, his actions that day might have been easier to understand. Before the shooting, he had started using PCP. There was also another secret people were not aware of, including Sappington himself. His mother had schizophrenia, and he was developing it as well.

Voices In His Head

On April 7th, 2001, Sappington was in his room, experiencing distress from the voices in his head. His PCP use and schizophrenia were ganging up on him. He heard a knock on his bedroom door; it was Terry T. Green. Twenty-five-year-old Green had been a long-time friend of Sappington's. As the two talked, Sappington had a hard time concentrating on their conversation. There was another voice drowning out Green's words. The voice told Sappington he needed to kill his friend.

Sappington told Green he needed help moving a box in the basement. When they were in the basement, Sappington waited till Green had his back turned away him and stabbed him with a hunting knife. Green screamed as he felt his own blood running down his shirt. Green stabbed him three more times; each stabbing motion sent blood spattering against the basement walls.

Sappington kneeled over Green's body and lapped up the blood as it flowed out of him until he heard a noise coming from outside the house. Alarmed that he would be caught, he hid the body in the basement, covering it with a tarp. When night came, he carried Green's body to his mother's car. He placed it in the trunk and drove off to a nightclub they had frequented. He found an unlocked car in the club's parking lot and placed Green's body on its backseat.

Police were alerted of Green's body on April 10th, when an employee of the nightclub was cleaning the parking lot. Sappington's voices did not tell him to kill Green; they just told him that he needed to kill someone. Green's misfortune was to be in the wrong place at the wrong time.

Twenty-two-year-old Michael Weaver Jr. was another longtime friend of Sappington's. He went to visit Sappington, who was in his backyard. Sappington's mother was out of the house. Sappington's voices told him he needed to eat human flesh. Weaver was joking with him as usual; however, Sappington could only hear his voices. Sappington had stolen a large kitchen knife from Weaver's home when he had visited that very morning. When Weaver was not looking, Sappington stabbed him in the back so hard the blade penetrated his chest.

Still alive, Weaver miraculously was able to escape. He ran to his car and drove off. Tragically, he did not make it. In his rapidly weakening condition, he lost control of his car and crashed into a light pole. A neighbor heard the crash and called the police. When they approached the vehicle, they found Weaver slumped over in the front seat.

Because Weaver got away from him, Sappington did not get the opportunity to drink his blood or taste his flesh. Unappeased, the voices in his head continued to torment him. He needed to satisfy them, and they would only be satisfied if he followed their command. On the very same day he killed Weaver, Sappington invited 21-one-year old Fred Alton Brown to his home. Brown was also a friend of Sappington's and would be his next victim.

When Brown came over, Sappington suggested they smoke "wet," which is a tainted form of marijuana. Marijuana dipped in a chemical, such as formaldehyde, dried, and then smoked. The two of them went down to his basement and started smoking the marijuana.

Smoking "wet" normally helped Sappington with his voices; however, not this time. He experienced the voices in their full potency as they commanded him to eat human flesh. Sappington chose Brown as his next target simply because he was available to him.

They got high. It was then that Sappington got up, went to the corner of the basement, and grabbed a gun he had hidden there. He shot Brown in the back, killing him instantly. Sappington could finally satisfy the commanding voices in his head. He could feast on human flesh.

Sappington cut a piece of flesh from Brown's leg and ate it, but there was a problem. He hated the taste. Determined to carry through with what he started, he took it upstairs to the kitchen and fried the piece of flesh. When the meat was cooked, he returned to the basement to eat it and drink Brown's blood. For the first time, he was able to appease the voices. Sappington dismembered Brown's body and hid the body parts in different locations throughout the city.

Got To Get Away

On April 10th, Sappington was feeling fearful again. He had realized what he had done and knew it was only a matter of time before he was captured for his crimes. He was walking away from his house when he saw the perfect opportunity. His neighbor, Anita

Washington, had just pulled in to her driveway after returning home from the grocery store. Sappington car jacked Washington's car. He got in the back seat and ordered her to drive him out of town. As she drove, Sappington repeatedly yelled out that he was a "dead man."

He eventually ordered Washington to pull over so he could drive; she was not driving fast enough for him. It was when she got out of the car to let Sappington drive that she escaped him by running away. She contacted the police and told them what had happened.

The police apprehended Sappington on April 11th. He confessed to all his crimes and took detectives to where he had disposed of the bodies.

He was charged with three counts of first-degree murder, one count of kidnapping, and aggravated burglary. He is serving life in prison without the chance of parole.

VII

Alex Kinyua

ON MAY 31ST, 2012, JARROD KINYUA SAT IN THE living room of his brother's Hartford home. His brother, Alexander, was taking a shower. A student at Maryland's Morgan University, Alexander was renting the townhouse while he attended school. Jarrod got up from the couch to walk around the house. When Jarrod passed the laundry room, something caught his attention. On top of the dryer, he noticed a blanket that was covering something and had a strong smell to it.

When he lifted the towel, he stood in a state of shock. Underneath the blanket was two tin dishes that contained a human head and two human hands! Distraught, Jarrod called his father,

Antony Kinyua, to tell him of his gruesome discovery. Antony told Jarrod he was on his way over to the townhouse. As Jarrod put down the phone, Alexander stepped out of the bathroom. Jarrod told him about the body parts, but Alexander told him that he was mistaken. Alexander told his brother what he had seen were animal parts.

Jarrod did not believe his brother's explanation and felt scared being around him. To his relief, he heard his father drive up outside. Jarrod bolted outside to his father. When Jarrod and his father went to the laundry room, the tin dishes and the body parts were gone. They heard water running in the basement. When they reached the basement, they caught Alexander hosing off the two tin dishes. Jarrod had uncovered more than a head and pair of hands. He had uncovered a dark secret that his brother was trying to hide. Morgan University had a cannibal for a student.

Major Crazy at Morgan

Alexander Kinyua was born on October 23rd, 1990, in Kenya. He had moved with his family to the United States and become an American citizen. Antony became a physics professor at Morgan University, while Alexander studied electrical engineering. Alexander rented a townhouse in Joppa, a town in Hartford County.

Kinyua was doing well at Morgan. He had a high grade-point average and was on track to graduate as a senior in the fall of 2012. Additionally, he was involved in the university's Reserve Officers Training Corps (RTOC) program. However, things started changing for him around 2011. He started to experience hallucinations and found himself in his own alternative universe.

He started talking about blood sacrifices and reptilian aliens planning to destroy the Earth. He also became obsessed with world cleansing, violence, and the end of the world. He would make his beliefs public by blogging about them, writing books, and even preaching. He believed he was a shaman with secret powers and preached about his philosophy every opportunity he could find. He once spoke about human sacrifices during an anti-hazing forum at school.

The following is an excerpt from one of his Facebook postings:

"Hear me out butchers: are you strong enough to endure ritual mass human sacrifices around the country and still be able to function as human beings? It's been all too tragic with the dual university shootings at Virginia Tech and other past university killings across the country. Now for a twist: ethnic cleansing is the policy, strategy, and tactics that will affect you, directly or indirectly in the coming months. This is the brutal basis, an evil and terrifying method of these death cults."

Besides his obsessive thinking about his philosophy, he was also becoming increasingly violent in his behavior. In December 2011, Kinyua visited the ROTC office on campus. Earlier that morning, he had experienced hallucinations, but he was determined to go to campus anyway. As he sat in the ROTC office, his hallucinations began to act up again. They convinced him other students had sabotaged his computer records and were conspiring to get him drunk so he would not be able to attend the school's football game. Kinyua became angered and started punching holes in the wall. He was immediately discharged from the ROTC.

Kinyua believed he was a warrior, sent to Earth to save it from reptilian aliens. He intentionally burned patterns into his arms, which he claimed to be tribal markings. He also got a tattoo of a "portal" inked on the top of his bald head. He started to collect weapons, including a machete and brass knuckles. The few male friends Kinyua had were asked by female students as to why they would hang around him. To the female students, he was 'creepy.'

On May 19th, 2012, 23-year-old Joshua Ceaser, had planned to attend a friend's graduation. He decided to spend some time and visit Kinyua's roommate. Kinyua knew the fact that Ceaser would be visiting. Kinyua's roommate, Kujoe Bonsafo Agyei-Kodie, would be late returning to the townhouse, so he would not be there to greet Ceaser.

Kinyua sat in a chair as he waited for Ceaser to arrive. In his hands, he had a baseball bat that had barbwire wrapped around it. His hallucinations told him that Ceaser was a threat to children. As he waited, he repeatedly told himself, "Somebody has to protect the kids. I gotta protect the kids." When Ceaser entered his townhouse, Kinyua proceeded to beat him with the bat.

Other students heard Ceaser's screams and rushed to see what was happening. When they arrived, they discovered Ceaser badly wounded on the floor and Kinyua standing above him with a knife. A group of students rushed Kinyua and pinned him to a wall as another student called 911. The vicious attack on Ceaser left him with a cognitive impairment and traumatic optic neuropathy.

Kinyua was arrested by campus police and charged with assault and reckless endangerment. While the prosecutor requested bail be denied, the court freed Kinyua on $220,000 bail. It would be a decision the court commissioner would live to regret!

The Roommate

On May 25th, 2012, Kinyua's roommate, 37-year-old Agyei-Kodie, arrived back to the townhouse. He had been introduced to Alexander through Antony, who had befriended him. He moved in with Alexander six weeks after meeting Antony. He also did not know about the incident with Ceaser.

He was feeling depressed because of a dark cloud that hung over his head. He faced deportation back to Ghana, due to him violating the terms of his visa. He had been accused of stalking a female student. He had come home early from campus so he could go to sleep and escape his problems.

Outside the townhouse, Kinyua was using a machete to cut some plants that were overgrown. It was then he experienced more hallucinations. He grew upset and angry as the voices told him that Agyei-Kodie was out to get him. He started cursing Agyei-Kodie and decided he had to do something about it. Kinyua marched into the townhouse and straight to Agyei-Kodie's room.

Standing over his sleeping roommate, Kinyua started hacking him with the machete. Agyei-Kodie let out a scream, but his screams quickly turned to silence. Kinyua disembodied and decapitated his roommate's body. A sudden urge led him to break open the rib cage, tear out his heart, and feast on it. He then smashed open the skull and started to consume the brain. Kinyua kept the head and hands but dumped the rest of the body in a dumpster behind the Towne Baptist Church, which was a mile away from the townhouse.

Father Turns In Son

On May 31st, Antony called the police to report what Jarrod had told him. He believed his son, which he could not do with Alexander. From what Antony saw in Jarrod's eyes, he knew that Alexander was up to something. Additionally, Agyei-Kodie's father had also called police to report him missing on May 25th.

Kinyua was arrested on May 31st at his home. At first, he denied any involvement, but he eventually confessed. He had no choice; police had found enough evidence. Because he was diagnosed with schizophrenia, he was committed to Clifton T. Perkins Hospital, a maximum-security psychiatric hospital, where he was to remain for the remainder of his life.

VIII

Otty Sanchez

IT WAS JULY 20TH, 2009, AND 33-YEAR-OLD OTTY Sanchez was being led out of Metropolitan Methodist Hospital by her sister. She was being discharged from Metropolitan the same day she'd arrived. Sanchez had pleaded with the hospital staff to hospitalize her, but they ignored her pleas. Instead, they gave her a referral to a clinic and called her sister to pick her up.

This all happened despite the insistence of her counselor, from the referring clinic, who stressed that Sanchez needed to be hospitalized. Her counselor believed she was exhibiting signs of postpartum psychosis. The hospital's mistake of releasing Sanchez would lead to horrifying consequences.

Starting Early

Born in 1976 (exact date not known), Sanchez grew up in San Antonio, Texas. She was raised by her mother; she never knew her father. From the time she was 5, Sanchez heard voices in her head. To make matters worse, her mother, aunt, and some cousins also heard voices. Sanchez lived with her grandmother, mother, sister, and two nieces. They lived in the north section of San Antonio.

As she got older, her voices became more frequent, making it difficult for her to function. Besides the voices, she also had memories of beatings and molestation she'd experienced by the men in her neighborhood, something she never told her mother about.

Rocky Times

The tension between her and her family became worse over the years. By the time she was a teenager, she had decided to leave home. Her hearing voices, having no privacy, and being a rebellious teenager, had all taken their toll.

Sanchez had seen some therapist about her voices, and she was able to obtain medication for it. Before 2008, San Antonio offered community outreach to those who were uninsured. Her problem was consistency. Being on her own, and with limited resources, she was not always able to make it to the clinic. Also, she only went when she felt that she needed it. She lacked a continuum of treatments, as do many people with mental illness who are struggling economically.

Tired of struggling, Sanchez decided to go to a school that offered a program for becoming a pharmacist assistant. It was at school that she met Scott Buchholtz, who was around her age. Buchholtz was also a student in the program, and the two quickly developed a relationship. It was a relationship doomed to failure. Sanchez did not tell Buchholtz she had schizophrenia, and Buchholtz had the same disease.

A Critical Moment

Sanchez moved in with Buchholtz, who lived with his parents. Their romance was short-lived. Their arguing and fighting were frequent; their relationship was very dysfunctional. Sanchez left Buchholtz and moved back with her family. Things were getting better for her and her family until things got even more complicated. Sanchez discovered she was pregnant. Though she was reluctant, she felt it was only right to return to Buchholtz. She stayed with him through her pregnancy, and things seemed to be getting better between them. He showed a real interest in the baby, which was born on June 30th.

All hopes for becoming a couple again, however, soon fell apart. Because of the birth, Sanchez did not want to take her medication, which resulted in her experiencing voices and drastic changes in her mood. Her emotional upset was complicated by the fact that she had developed an infection after giving birth and had to use a catheter. Things between the couple became volatile again. Two weeks after giving birth, Sanchez took the baby and returned to her mother's home.

Communication Breakdown

Sanchez was slipping into depression, and the voices were becoming rampant. She knew she needed help, especially because her baby depended on her. She went to a clinic and saw a counselor on July 20th. She explained to the counselor that she was having delusions that other women were breastfeeding her baby and seeing the faces of other babies being transposed on her baby's face.

The counselor was concerned and suspected that Sanchez was experiencing postpartum depression. Understanding that Sanchez required immediate attention, she called Metropolitan Methodist hospital. The person who answered the phone at Metropolitan Methodist did not want to take any medical information from the counselor, leaving the counselor no choice but to have EMS (Emergency Medical Services) convey the information to the hospital when they got there.

When Sanchez arrived at Metropolitan Methodist, she was left waiting for 20 minutes before anyone attended her. When the medical staff did see her, they conducted medical tests on her for the next three hours, tests that had nothing to do with her mental condition.

When she did receive a mental evaluation, it was done by a counselor, not a psychiatrist. Her history was never discussed, and it was determined that hospitalization was not needed. While they believed she was experiencing hallucinations and delusions, the hospital staff never received the information she may be suffering from postpartum depression. Sanchez was given a referral to a clinic and released to her sister.

Sanchez was left alone to deal with the voices by herself. In late 2008, funding for mental health care was slashed and Sanchez, like many other low-income people, no longer had the community outreach for mental services. Because she could not hold a job, she had no insurance.

By 5:00 a.m.

It was 4:30 a.m., on July 26th, that the voices took her to a nightmarish extreme. Her voices told her that the devil had taken over her son, that her baby was going to be the apocalypse. They told her, "eat his insides…that she was a harlot because she had committed adultery and that there was a demon in her stomach." The voices also told her she had to eat her baby by 5:00 a.m. By doing this, her baby would no longer be possessed.

While the rest of her family members were fast asleep, she got out of her bed, grabbed a large kitchen knife, and walked over to her baby's crib. Raising her knife, she repeatedly stabbed her baby. She mutilated her son's genitals, decapitated him, and ate his brain. The taste of her son's flesh caused her to throw-up, but her voices demanded that she continue eating him. Her horrified cousin walked into the room and saw the mayhem. She called 911 as Sanchez wailed in anguish for what she had done.

Sanchez grabbed the knife and plunged it into her own stomach. Sanchez was arrested on the same day and was found not guilty by reason of insanity and committed to a state institution.

IX

Tyree Lincoln Smith

IT WAS A WINTER EVENING IN BRIDGEPORT, Connecticut. Thirty-five-year-old Tyree Lincoln Smith sought refuge from the snow and cold. Homeless, he decided to spend the night at the abandoned and burned out Riverside Apartments, where he'd grown up as a child. Though the building was boarded up, he found access to the building. As Smith slept, 43-year-old Angel Gonzales also entered the Riverside Apartments. Like Smith, he was also homeless. Gonzales' decision to seek refuge there would cost him his life.

Spiraling Downward

Smith was born on January 11th, 1977, in Bridgeport. His parents, Cheryl Rabb and Adolph Smith, were not married when he was born. Rabb was 18-years-old, and Smith was 21-years-old when Tyree was born. His parents got married when he turned seven years old and moved to the Riverside Apartments, located on Olson Drive. The three-story structure was a public housing project and would later be the setting for a horrific murder.

When he turned 12, Smith and his family moved to the nearby city of Ansonia. He attended Ansonia High School, where his teachers considered him to be an above-average student. Smith appeared to be a normal teenager until he reached the eleventh grade. It was at that time that he started to hear voices.

Smith was no longer able to concentrate on his school work and dropped out of school on September 8th, 1994. Though his voices were becoming worse, it did not stop him from trying to get his life back on track. He enrolled in the Job Corps, where he helped high school students learn a trade. After a while, he had trouble holding that position and moved to California to become a model. While he was in California, his voices became worse and he spent a short period at Yale Psychiatric Institute.

Because his plans to become a model did not turn out, he returned to Ansonia. Those who knew him saw a major change in him when he came back. He had become reckless in the way he lived his life. He slept with different women, from which he fathered two sons. He increased his consumption of alcohol, neglected his hygiene, and could not hold a job. He worked briefly in a coffee shop and as a manager for a video game store until he stopped working completely.

The thing most people did not know about Scott was that he heard voices. They were also becoming worse. One of the frequent messages his voices gave him was that he needed to kill people. Scott started blogging about his growing obsession with death.

The following is a post from his Facebook account:

"Devouring your flesh. Smelling your bodies burning in a heap. I hate the day they created you filthy humans. There. That's what been on my mind since a child. Happy?"

Not only were his voices becoming worse, but his cognitive abilities also began to degrade. Neighbors saw him doing bizarre things like walking in the snow in only his underwear and a blank expression on his face.

In July 2011, Smith visited a CVS pharmacy, in Fairfield, to fill a prescription. While shopping, his voices started acting up again. As he walked among the store aisles, he noticed one of the store employees had left a box cutter on top of one of the boxes he was unpacking. Smith took the box cutter and slit his wrist. As blood streamed from his wound, he became light-headed and collapsed on the floor. Medics took him to St. Vincent's Medical Center Behavioral Health Services in Westport.

St. Vincent's discharged him when he stabilized; however, his mental health went downhill quickly. He did not take care of himself, nor did anyone intervene. By law, he had to be a danger to himself or others for him to be hospitalized. In six months, Scott would meet those criteria in the most horrific way.

Do Not Disturb!

In December 2011, Scott took refuge for the night inside the abandoned Riverside Apartments. He made his way up to the third floor, reducing the possibilities he would be detected by other homeless people. With him, he had an ax, which he kept hidden inside the apartment. He also had a bottle of Sake for him to drink when he needed to clear his mind.

Forty-three-year-old Angel Gonzales walked up to the third floor of the Riverside Apartment to escape the cold. He came across the sleeping Scott and woke him up. Fueled by his anger and the commands of his voices, Scott grabbed his hatchet and attacked Gonzales. His lethal blows left Gonzales's mutilated body lying in a pool of blood. He ate Gonzales's brain, as prompted by his voices so that he could better understand human behavior. He then ate Gonzales's eyes so that he could develop a greater vision of the spiritual realm. He would later tell the authorities that the eyes tasted like oysters.

When he was done, Scott went over to his cousin's house and told her what he had just done. He was holding the bloody ax, and his clothes were stained with blood. Having confessed to his cousin, he walked off and went to a Subway restaurant because he was still hungry. Scott's cousin called the police to advise them of what had just happened.

Police located Scott smoking outside the Riverside Apartments and arrested him. He confessed to the murder and showed them where the body was.

On November 11th, he was found not guilty by reason of insanity and committed to Whiting Forensic Division of Connecticut Valley Hospital in Middletown.

X

Joseph Oberhansley

ON JULY 21, 2014, TAMMY JO BLANTON APPEARED at a Clark County courthouse to pay her boyfriend's bail. Joseph Oberhansley was being held for failing to stop for an Indiana police officer. He had led police on a slow-speed chase across two states. Judge Weber had set bail at $25,000, but a strange thing happened. The prosecutor negotiated a reduction in the bail. The bail was reduced to $5,000. Blanton was able to get her boyfriend out by paying only $500.00. That the judge willing to lower bail to $5,000 proved to be a fatal mistake that would cost Blanton her life. It also allowed Oberhansley to escape the criminal justice system one more time.

Family Darkness

Oberhansley was born March 29th, 1981, in Indiana. His mother, Brenda Self, and his sister, Alesha Olsen, remember him as a sweet child, as did his cousin, Misty Morgan. His family never even heard him swear. All that would change when he became a teenager. That was when Oberhansley experienced the dark side of his family. His half-brother killed himself, and his father died from a drug overdose. His sweet childhood came to an end. The brightness in his life gradually became eclipsed by his own demons. The death of his half-brother and his father were the catalyst for the unleashing of a monster.

To put his painful memories behind him, Oberhansley and his girlfriend, Sabrina Elder, moved from Indiana to Utah. They lived with his mother and sister, who had a home in the suburbs of Salt Lake City. Unfortunately for Oberhansley, he was not able to run away from his past by moving to another state. In December 1998, Oberhansley became fearful. He was 17-years-old, his life going nowhere, and he had gotten Elder pregnant. Sabrina gave birth to a baby boy on December 9th. Their new son was named Joseph Oberhansley, Jr.

On the night of December 14th, Oberhansley got together with some friends and got high on meth. He was trying to escape the deep-seated fear that is consuming him, a fear he had not shared with anyone. He was afraid of life. He felt powerless and was afraid of losing anyone else.

Extreme Violence

He returned to his mother's home high as a kite. Elder, the baby, and his mother were in the living room watching television. When Elder saw the condition he was in, she became angry with him. He was a father now. How could he behave this way! An argument ensued when he pulled out a gun from his pants. Elder and his mother screamed and begged him to put the gun down. Oberhansley finally felt powerful. He shot Elder repeatedly. His mother threw herself on top of Elder to shield her. He was not deterred a bit. He shot his mother when his sister ran into the room. She grabbed the baby and ran for the front door; he fired at her but missed.

His sister and son barely escaped with their lives. Elder was killed, while his mother was seriously wounded. Understanding that he had unleashed a demon from within him, he put the gun underneath his chin and fired a single shot. Oberhansley's suicide attempt failed as doctors were able to save him. However, his survival only made him even more dangerous. The bullet he had fired to end his life was lodged in the frontal lobe of his brain. He damaged the part of his brain that affects personality, decision-making, and self-control, all things he'd struggled with before the suicide attempt.

Oberhansley received a sweetheart of a deal when his attorney managed to get him a plea deal. He was sentenced to manslaughter and attempted murder. He was sentenced to 12 years, paroled in 2012. As part of the agreement, he would be able to serve out his parole in Indiana, which he considered home. Upon being released from prison, he moved to Jeffersonville.

On March 10th, 2013, Oberhansley was relaxing at Johnny D's, a bar in Jeffersonville. A loner, he frequently went to the bar to play darts and be around other people. It was on this date he met a woman who was having a drink. He found the woman attractive and the two of them spent time talking. He could not believe his luck when the woman invited him back to her apartment, located right above another local bar. The name of that bar was Slammers.

When they reached her apartment, they wasted no time. They stripped their clothes off in the living room and went to her bedroom to have sex. What Oberhansley did not realize was the woman's invitation had been a trap. While she was having sex with him, her boyfriend was going through his clothing, searching for items to steal.

The boyfriend found a few worthwhile items to take, hid them in his car, and then went back to the apartment. Grabbing a baseball bat, he entered the bedroom. Acting as though he was a jealous boyfriend who had just caught him in bed with his girlfriend, he hit Oberhansley in the back of the head. What the boyfriend did not understand was that he was messing with the wrong man. In a sudden surge of power and fury, Oberhansley charged the boyfriend, who took off.

The boyfriend ran in the bathroom and locked the door to protect himself. His attempts to escape Oberhansley were futile. Oberhansley broke down the bathroom door, grabbed the boyfriend by the neck, and began choking him.

The bartender at Slammers heard the commotion and called the police. When the police arrived at the apartment, they had to taser him twice to get Oberhansley off the boyfriend, who was barely alive. Oberhansley was charged on July 29th with strangulation, aggravated battery, and resisting arrest. He was sent to the Clark County Jail. In a breakdown of the justice system, he was released on $1,000 bail, as the judge did not realize that Oberhansley was on parole from Utah. His mother's step-father bailed him out.

She Stood by Her Man

In the spring of 2014, Oberhansley met a woman named Tammy Jo Blanton. Blanton was 46-years-old and lived in Jeffersonville. The two started dating, a fatal mistake for Blanton. Though Oberhansley told her about his past, he only told her in general terms and indicated he had left his troubles behind him. Blanton never understood the details of his past.

Though she loved Oberhansley, her view of him would soon change. She began noticing Oberhansley's controlling tendencies. He was trying to keep her isolated by arguing with her when she wanted to be with her friends, and he monitored her social media accounts. Though her friends expressed their concerns about him, Blanton remained with him.

On July 21st, Oberhansley was arrested again. Police spotted him driving recklessly, and he refused to pull over. He led the police on a slow chase through two states. Ironically, Indiana authorities learned from Utah's parole department that his parole had expired on the same date he was arrested. Blanton bailed out her boyfriend on July 3st. If she had never paid the $500, she would most likely be alive today.

Rejection Kills

Blanton could no longer deal with Oberhansley's controlling manner. In early September, she broke up with him and had the locks changed to her house. For Oberhansley, her rejection was more than he could handle. On September 11th, Oberhansley drove to Blanton's home in the late evening. When he arrived, he grabbed a large hunting knife and exited his car. Though Blanton had changed the locks, he knew of a window she left open to let in the fresh evening air.

He crawled through the window and walked down the dark hallway to her bedroom. Blanton was fast asleep. Grabbing his knife, he started savagely stabbing her as she let out a scream. He was relentless as he repeatedly stabbed her in her head, neck, and chest. He tore open her chest cavity and used a jigsaw to cut open her skull. He grabbed her heart and ripped it out of her, tearing off pieces of her lungs as he did so. He also removed chunks of her brain. Grabbing the body parts, he brought them to the kitchen, cooked them, and then ate them. When he was done, he returned to her bedroom, grabbed her body, and carried it to the bathroom. He placed her mutilated body in the bathtub and covered it up with a tarp.

The next day, Police received a call from her employer, stating that Blanton never arrived at work. Police also received a call from Oberhansley's mother, who told them her son was very emotional and upset with his girlfriend.

The police went over to her home to investigate. When they arrived, they saw splatters of blood outside her front door, where Oberhansley had exited. When police entered the residence, they found an alarming sight. In the kitchen trash was a skillet, a plate, and a pair of tongs, all stained with blood. They discovered her body in the bathroom.

When police questioned Oberhansley, he confessed to the crime.

Attorneys argued that he was not competent to stand trial.

In October 2017, he was deemed competent to stand trial, but a trial date has not yet been set.

XI

Gregory Scott Hale

JUNE 8, 2014, WILL BE A DATE THAT WILL ALWAYS haunt Charles Hyder. That was the day he received a call from his ex-wife, Lisa Hyder.

Lisa, a thirty-seven-year-old store clerk, was finishing up her shift at the liquor store she worked at, which was located in Manchester, Tennessee. She asked him if he could pick her up. Charles informed her he was some distance away and told her to wait for him.

No Answer

When he was en route to pick Lisa up, he called her to let her know he was on the way. Lisa never answered her phone. Thinking she already got a ride back, he drove home and called her again. Still, she did not answer. To his horror, Charles would later discover his wife did get a ride home that day. It would also be the last day of her life.

My Hero

Thirty-seven-year-old Gregory Scott Hale lived with his parents in Summitville, a rural of Tennessee. The neighbors knew enough of Hale to cause them uneasiness. Hale had moved back in with his parents when he lost his job at the meat processing plant. He was terminated for taking blood, bones, and the eyes of slaughtered animals home with him.

Taking home animal parts was only one of the bizarre habits Hale demonstrated. He idolized serial killer Richard Ramirez, popularly known as the Night Stalker. In the summer of 1989, Ramirez went on a killing and raping spree in Southern California. He was convicted of 13 murders, five attempted murderers, 11 sexual assaults, and 14 burglaries.

Hale inspired to be like Ramirez and obsessively read Ramirez's "manifesto."

When Ramirez died earlier that year, Hale wrote on Facebook:

"R.I.P. Night Stalker....Wish I could have met U..."

He frequently blogged and posted pictures on Facebook to share his obsession with Satan worship, weapons, cannibalism, and Ramirez. Hale also posted pictures of himself dressed in black, armed with large knives and other weapons. He also posted pictures holding venomous snakes and the heavy metal group Slayer.

He also posted the following comments:

"I hug the people I hate so I know how big to dig their hole in my backyard."

"If someone were to become a cannibal and eat a vegetarian, would the vegetarian taste like that fake soy meat?"

Deadly Encounter

Hale was driving through Manchester when he stopped off at a liquor store to get some beer. When he left the store, he noticed an attractive woman waiting on the corner. That woman was Lisa Hyder, who had just gotten off work. Hyder had recently separated from her husband. When they had been together, they had lived in the suburbs of Chattanooga, with their six children. They had separated because of her alcoholism. Her refusal to get help eventually created a breaking point in their marriage. She also had another demon to deal with; she had ovarian cancer.

Hyder was staying with friends in Manchester and was waiting for her ex-husband to pick her up. Hale offered to bring her home. She hesitated at first but was getting tired waiting. As they drove, Hyder noticed he was not following the directions she gave him. Hale told her that he needed to make a stop at his home.

When they arrived at his home, he invited her inside. She was hesitant until he mentioned they could have a few drinks before taking off again to bring her home. Hyder agreed. She did not have the strength to put up with all the stress she was experiencing in her life and wanted a drink.

Hale got the fireplace going and sat down next to her. He poured her a drink, and they started to talk about each other's lives. The effects of sharing each other's stories, the fire, and the alcohol came together to make her feel comfortable with Hale. Hale could detect this and moved in closer to her. They had a long kiss, and Hale suggested they go to bed.

After having sex, they lay in bed. When Hyder fell asleep, Hale got out of bed, went to his closet, and grabbed his machete. Standing over her sleeping body, Hale swung the machete with a hard, downward motion that caused the sharp blade to drive through her torso. She let out a scream of pain when he swung at her again and again.

Looking at the horrific results of his actions, Hale felt a great sense of pleasure. He had accomplished the kind of deed that his hero, Ramirez, was known for. The bedsheets were soaked in blood as it flowed from her deep gashes. His bedroom walls and carpet were splattered in red.

Hale disembodied and decapitated Hider's body. He placed her head and hands in one bucket, and her feet in another one. Smiling with pride, he picked the flesh from the body parts and began to eat them. He even used his phone to take a picture of the buckets filled with flesh. He decided to bury the rest of her body in his parent's backyard, which had a burn pit. It was the perfect place to bury a body. Though Hale wanted to be like Ramirez, he was not experienced in committing crimes. He made an unbelievable mistake.

Hale went to one of his neighbors and asked if he could borrow his backhoe. The mistake he made was the comment he made to the neighbor. He told his neighbor he needed the backhoe to bury a body!

His neighbor called the police, who arrived at Hale's home and arrested him. They found Hyder's body and the pails at the burn pit. Hale had no choice but to confess to his crime. He was charged with first-degree murder and the abuse of a corpse.

While many thought Hale was odd, no one could have imagined he would ever commit such a heinous crime. As a neighbor stated: "I don't know what to think that this kid I've known for 28 years could do something this gruesome."

Caught Just In Time?

A psychiatrist familiar with the case stressed the significance of catching Hale. He stated that Hale was in the beginning stages of learning how to kill. If he had not been caught, he most likely would have gone on to kill more people and had most likely rehearsed in his mind how to kill women by stalking them and imagining how to rape, kill, or capture them.

Hale was arraigned on June 23rd, where he pled guilty to first-degree murder. He was sentenced to life in prison without the possibility of parole.

XII

Joe Metheny

THE HUGE FRAME OF JOE METHENY SAT BEHIND his roadside barbecue stand as he waited for customers to come by. At 450 pounds, Metheny was surprisingly quick as he rose up to his feet to greet an approaching customer. The customer ordered a pork barbecue sandwich. Taking a bite of the sandwich, the customer nodded approvingly and walked back to his car.

Looking at his Tupperware storage containers, he saw that he was running low on what he referred to as his "special meat." An evil grin appeared on his face when he realized that he would have to replenish his supply.

Metheny had a secret recipe to make his barbecue sandwiches, for it contained an ingredient that his customers were unaware of. This ingredient blended perfectly with beef or pork.

That evening, Metheny closed-up his stand and drove back to his trailer. Upon arriving home, he grabbed his ax and took off in his car. He was off to get more of his "special meat." What his customers did not know was the barbecue they were eating contained human flesh.

It all started in July 1994. Metheny, a truck driver, had returned home after a long trip on the road. He and his wife lived in the slums of south Baltimore. He moved to South Baltimore after returning from a brief stint in the military service, where he started using heroin.

When he arrived at his apartment, he encountered an event that would bring him to the breaking point. His wife and his six-year-old son were gone! That they were missing was traumatic for him, but it was not surprising. His wife had a drug problem and often hung out with other drug users, spending a lot of time on the streets. Finding himself in an empty apartment sent him into a deep-seated rage. Being alone was a nemesis that followed him throughout his life.

Metheny was born in 1955 in West Virginia. His parents and five siblings lived in poverty. A laborer, his father was an alcoholic and neglected his family's needs. The family later moved to Essex, an unincorporated community in Baltimore, Maryland. His father was killed in a car crash when Metheny was six. To take care of her children, his mother had to work multiple jobs.

In 1975, his oldest brother committed suicide. All these experiences left Metheny feeling vulnerable and alone. Perhaps that is why he became involved with heroin in the service. Since he'd left the service, Metheny had no contact with his mother. He was trying to escape the ghosts of his past, the feeling of vulnerability and loneliness. But his past caught up with him. He found himself alone once again. He was not just alone; his son had been taken from him.

In August 1994, six months after discovering that his wife and son had left him, Metheny found out the details of what happened to them. His wife had found a boyfriend and moved in with him. Her new boyfriend was also heavily involved in drugs. Further, his wife had been arrested for a drug offense. Since Metheny had a criminal record of assault, Child Protective Services had taken custody of the son and placed him in foster care.

The rage he felt when he discovered this information sent his rage through the roof. Metheny grabbed his ax and stormed out of his apartment. He was going to get even with those who robbed him of his son, and he had a hunch of where he could find them. He got in his car and drove off.

Homeless people, prostitutes, and drug addicts frequently hung out under the bridge that crossed the Patapsco River. Metheny pulled up to the entrance of the bridge, got out of his car, and walked down the hillside toward the bottom of the bridge. When he got there, he saw two homeless men. One of them was lying on an old mattress. His wife was nowhere in sight. He roughed up the two homeless men and asked for information as to where his wife was.

The two men explained to Metheny that they did not know his wife and pleaded for him to leave them alone. In his anger, Metheny swung his ax at the men. Being six-feet tall and 450 pounds, the power behind his swings was enormous. The first man was killed instantly and collapsed to the ground. The second man was severely wounded. Metheny repeatedly swung his ax until the second man was dead. Chopping them to pieces, he threw their remains in the river.

There was something about killing those two men that awakened something in him. For the first time in his life, he felt powerful. He felt the desire for a repeat performance. He wanted to kill again. The anger he held for his wife defined for him who his next targets would be. They would be women, especially those who were drug users or prostitutes. In his mind, they were like his wife; they were worthless. For him, killing would be his revenge.

A few nights later, Metheny went back to the bridge. He came across a prostitute, who was doing drugs. He told her he wanted sex and invited her under the bridge. Once there, he strangled and beat her, after which he disposed of her body in the river. A few hours later, he did the same with another prostitute. However, he encountered a problem after killing the second prostitute.

When he was about to dump her body in the river, he saw a black man fishing. The man had witnessed the murder. Metheny grabbed an iron pipe and attacked the fisherman, killing him. He dumped both bodies in the river. He had killed three people in one night and enjoyed it. Though he was scared about being caught, the knowledge he killed them gave him a grotesque sense of pride. Fortunately for him, the bodies would never be found. He had committed the perfect crime. However, he did not have the same luck with his first two murders.

Around three weeks after the killings of the two homeless men, the Baltimore police arrested him for the killings. He was jailed in the Baltimore city jail and put on trial. One week into his trial, the murder charges against him were dismissed due to a lack of evidence.

In 1995, Metheny walked out of jail a free man. However, he was homeless and without a job. The company he worked for, Joe Stein & Son Pallet Co., had let him go while he was incarcerated.

He went back to his employer, begging them to take him back. His employer eventually gave in to his persuasion and rehired him. His new position would be as a forklift driver for $7.00 an hour. His employer also let him stay in an abandoned trailer on company grounds.

In the same year, his double murder case was dismissed, Metheny came across 45-year-old Cathy Ann Magaziner, a prostitute. Just looking at her sickened him. Like his wife, he saw her as being a useless piece of trash. He told her he was interested in her services and brought her to his trailer. As soon as they entered the trailer, he unleashed a brutal beating on her. Magaziner screamed, which caused him to give out a cruel laugh. He knew there was no one around to hear her screaming.

Badly beaten and barely conscious, he grabbed an extension cord and strangled her. He then stabbed her repeatedly, even though she was dead already. He dragged her body out of the trailer and buried her in a shallow grave he had dug near his trailer. A few months later, he dug her up, decapitated her, and had sex with her skull.

In 1996, twenty-six-year-old Kimberly Lynn Spicer met the same fate as Magaziner. Like Magaziner, she also was a prostitute lured into Metheny's trailer. She also was beaten, strangled, and stabbed. Unlike Magaziner, he did not decapitate her. Metheny wanted to bury her as well but had difficulty digging the grave. He asked a friend to assist him. His friend refused to help him, so Metheny hid her body under a neighboring trailer. What Metheny did not realize was that his friend had called the police. The police never followed up with him.

There was one other thing that Metheny did to the two prostitutes, and he had done this before he disposed of their bodies. He carved off pieces of their flesh and placed them in Tupperware containers, which he froze.

Later that same year, Metheny noticed that he was running low again on his "special meat" for his open-pit barbecue stand. That night, he managed to lure another prostitute, Rita Kemper, to his trailer. Like the previous prostitutes, Metheny started off by giving her a savage beating.

However, that is when all similarity ends. When he was not looking, Kemper ran out of the trailer, scaled a fence, and made her way to a payphone to call the police.

When the police arrived at Metheny's trailer, he was waiting for them. He had no desire to run. He also confessed to his crime against Kemper.

During interrogation, Metheny claimed he had killed ten people. Authorities could not locate evidence to charge him with the murders he claimed to have committed, except one. They found enough evidence to charge him with the death of twenty-eight-year-old Tori Lyn Ingrassia.

During the trial, Metheny admitted to all charges against him and showed no remorse. In fact, he enjoyed shocking the jury and the families of the victims by proudly telling the details of his crimes and using obscene language when referring to his victims.

Metheny begged jurors to give him the death penalty. He was indicted on three counts of murder for the deaths of Kimberly Spicer, Toni Lynn Ingrassia, and Catherine Magaziner.

When the jury reached their verdict, they found him guilty on all counts, and he was given the death penalty in 1998. During the penalty stage of his trial, the court overthrew the death sentence for Magaziner. His final sentence was two life sentences without the possibility of parole.

In 2017, 62-year-old Metheny was found dead in his cell at Western Correctional Institution.

Conclusion

IT WOULD BE EASY TO DISMISS THE INDIVIDUALS profiled in this book as being crazy or evil. However, to do so does not shine a light on the potential causes and what could have been done to help prevent these horror stories from happening.

Stanley Dean Baker and Antron Singleton used drugs; PCP.

Albert Fentress, Alex Kinyua, Otty Sanchez, Alex Kinyua, and Tyree Lincoln Smith all had a form of mental illness.

Marc Sappington had mental illness and used PCP.

Joseph Oberhansley had mental illness and had self-inflicted brain damage.

Omaima Aree Nelson had PTSD. We are waiting to find out what the cause was behind the murders committed by Austin Harrouff and Gregory Scott Hale, though Harrouff is suspected of suffering from mental illness.

We will never know the infliction of Metheny since he passed away.

It's not to say that using drugs or having mental illness leads to murder and cannibalism. Many people who have experienced either of these conditions and did not commit such heinous crimes.

However, some people have something about them, which, when combined with mental illness or drug use, leads to them committing the extreme behavior explored in this book.

Sometimes, when people are pushed to the extreme, they resort to committing extreme acts. In 1845, English captain John Franklin led his crew to explore the Arctic. The ship of 129 men mysteriously vanished. A search for the lost expedition later led to the discovery of the crewmen's graves, some of which showed signs that cannibalism had occurred.

In 1846, the Donner Party, a group of American explorers, became stranded in the Sierra Nevada mountains. They had eaten the bodies of their team members who had not made it.

The individuals profiled in this book were also pushed to the extreme. In their own private madness, they could no longer take it. The horrors these killer cannibals committed, and the pain they left on the victim's families, will be repeated in the future. They will be repeated by other individuals who are also pushed to the extreme unless we learn as a society to support those who are hanging by the end of their rope.

List of Twelve Volume 4

12 Terrifying True Crime Murder Cases

Introduction

WELCOME TO VOLUME 4 OF THE TRUE CRIME Series. In this volume, you will be treated to a look into the world of spree killers.

The U.S. Bureau of Justice Statistics defines a spree killer as someone who kills two or more people in multiple locations. Though their victims may have been killed in different locations, the killings of spree killers are considered one event because of the lack of a cooling down period.

In this volume of True Crime, you will get the background history of each killer, details of their grisly crimes, and, when applicable, information on their trial and sentencing.

In this volume, you will read about:

- Jiverly Antares Wong: a Vietnamese immigrant whose frustration with his unemployment spilled over, leading him to shoot up the Binghamton's American Civic Association.
- Priscilla Ford: a 51-year-old woman who intentionally barreled down a Reno sidewalk in her Lincoln Continental and mowed down a crowd of pedestrians.
- Adam Lanza: a 20-year-old shooter behind the Sandy Hook Elementary School massacre.
- Brenda Spencer: a 16-year-old girl whose nightmarish home environment led her to become the first mass shooter of a U.S. school.
- Jared Lee Loughner: an Arizona man whose downward spiral into mental illness led him to unleash a barrage of bullets during a political event.
- Seung Hui Cho: a Korean immigrant whose bizarre behavior at school led him to go on a bloody rampage at Virginia Tech.
- Charles Joseph Whitman: from being an Eagle Scout, altar boy, and a Marine, to becoming the man who carried out a

bloodbath from his perch in the tower at the University of Texas.

- Mark Barton: day trader without a conscious, who shot up the financial firm he worked at after suffering a major financial loss.
- Jennifer San Marco: one of the few female spree killers. San Marco's escalating erratic behavior led her to seek revenge on a neighbor, then at the mail processing center where she worked.
- Michael Kenneth McLendon: a small-town Alabama man whose life was going nowhere. The answer to his dilemma: gun down his family and relatives.
- Christopher Harper-Mercer: tormented by his own mind, he entered his writing-composition course at Umpqua Community College and gunned down the class full of students.
- Dana Ewell: an arrogant and privileged college student, he wanted to be a multi-millionaire. When his millionaire father threatened his inheritance, he hired his roommate to execute his family.

We all have a fight or flight response. Get ready to read about individuals who got tired of fleeing and decided to fight back in an extreme way.

I
Jiverly Antares Wong

JIVERLY ANTARES WONG SAT QUIETLY AS HE waited for his number to be called at the Binghamton American Civic Association in New York. He was there to apply for benefits, as he was recently laid off from his job at the Shop-Vac Factory, which was closing its plant in Binghamton.

In South Vietnam, Wong could barely speak English even though he had been living in the United States for almost ten years.

His number was finally called, and Wong walked up to the window of the benefits representative. Seeing that Wong was having a difficult time expressing himself in English, she gave him a phone number that assisted Chinese and Japanese speakers. Wong became insulted and told her that he was Vietnamese and stormed out of the building.

What that representative did not know was that Wong would come back and catapult the Binghamton American Civic Center into international news as the site of a mass shooting.

Resistant to Change

Wong was born on December 8th, 1967. He was the second oldest of four children. His family moved to the United States from Vietnam in July 1990, when he was 22. They were able to come to America because of their refugee status. He became an American citizen in November 1995.

While the rest of his family were able to integrate into American society, Wong did not. Among the things that frustrated him was finding work and the language barrier; he did not want to learn to speak English. Because of this, he found his employment opportunities limited.

Of Pride, Secrecy, and Conspiracies

After gaining citizenship, the family moved to Ontario, Canada, where they lived for a few years before moving to upstate

New York. Wong moved to Inglewood, California in 2000. He believed he would feel more at home in the Los Angeles area because of its Korean community. Over the next 20 years, he would frequently move between Los Angeles and New York.

He rented a studio apartment close to Los Angeles Airport. His only window offered a view of a brick wall. For seven years, he lived there and worked for a company that made sushi, earning $9.00 an hour. He led a quiet life and did not socialize, as he was an introvert and very secretive, so secretive that he got married and did not tell his family. The marriage lasted seven years.

There were two things that Wong had strong feelings about: making his parents proud, and guns. Because of his culture, he grew up believing that he needed to be able to provide for his parents and family, even though they lived in New York. The pressure he was facing was because his parents and siblings were more successful than he was. They had assimilated into their community and could speak English reasonably well. He struggled with his English and could barely support himself; he had been arrested for passing a bad check. He also had an encounter with the police when he experienced a minor traffic accident. From these two incidents, Wong developed a paranoia about the police, believing they were conspiring to get him.

Struggling to make it in Los Angeles, Wong decided to move back to Binghamton and live with his parents. The Wong family lived in a single-family home, located in Union. It was a modest house that was home to his parents, his sister, and his niece, who was just an infant.

Wong found work at the Shop-Vac Factory in the village of Endicott. Though he had a job, he continued to struggle when trying to communicate with others, causing continuing frustration for him. His way of relieving stress was to go to the gun range and practice shooting; he would spend hours there. He became a skilled shooter and was able to hit a target 50-feet away. His weapon of choice was a semiautomatic Beretta pistol with a laser sight.

The Bottom Drops Out

In 2008, the U.S. economy faced its worst financial crisis since the Great Depression. Shop-Vac closed its factory, and Wong, along with his co-workers, was laid off.

Binghamton's American Civic Association (ACA) offers a wide range of services to the local immigrant community. It assists immigrants in attaining citizenship, as well as offering classes for learning English and cultural support.

While searching for employment, Wong went to ACA to apply for unemployment benefits. They recommended he take their course to learn English. Wong agreed and attended classes, but he did not speak to anyone.

Wong continued to struggle to find work. He was making it on $200 a week, which came from his unemployment benefits. On April 2nd, 2009, Wong went to the ACA to renew his benefits. When the representative advised him of the phone number for Chinese and Japanese speakers, he grew irate. He was Vietnamese. He was 42 and living with his parents when he should have been supporting them. He stormed out of the building.

Friday, April 3rd, 2009, Wong had an appointment at an employment center, where a counselor was working with him to find a job. Wong did not attend his appointment; he was too frustrated. Wong had other plans. Instead, he got his two Beretta pistols, a bulletproof vest, and drove back to the ACA, arriving around 10:30 a.m.

He pulled up to the rear of the building and parked in front of the rear entrance to create a barricade. He then exited his car and walked to the front entrance. Wong entered the building and, without a word, began shooting. He fired at anyone he saw. His first targets were two receptionists.

One receptionist was shot in the head, and the second one was shot in the abdomen. She played dead as she fell under her desk. She had the foresight to call 911. 61-year-old receptionist, Shirley DeLucia, remained on the line as she kept the 911 operator informed of what was happening as they waited for the police to arrive.

Wong continued to move around the building as he made his way to the classrooms where they taught English. He filled the classroom with gunfire as he relentlessly fired off shots. There was not one person in the classroom who was not hit. Some people avoided Wong's detection and hid in the basement. When he heard sirens approaching, Wong killed himself.

In three minutes, he had fired off 99 rounds. 13 people were killed, excluding Wong, while four others were injured.

II
Priscilla Ford

AS 51-ONE- YEAR OLD PRISCILLA FORD SAT BY HER attorney in the Reno courtroom, they waited for the jury to file in. The 5'4" black woman looked like anything but a hardcore criminal. Weighing in at 125 pounds, with brown, shoulder-length hair combed back, Ford's grandmotherly looks made her seem out of place.

The jury took their seats, and the jury foreman stood up to read the verdict. They found her guilty on six counts of murder and 23 counts of attempted murder. Ford's face had remained expressionless throughout the proceeding. The court officer handcuffed her and took her way.

She was about to become the only woman on Nevada's death row.

A Teacher's Descent into Darkness

Born February 10th, 1929 in Barren Springs, Michigan, Ford's life was one of inspiration to all who knew her until she became the perpetrator of the 1980 Thanksgiving Day Massacre.

In 1957, with only a high school diploma, she started teaching in a one-room schoolhouse in the city of Dowagiac. The school board was nervous having her as she was the first black person ever hired. Their concerns gradually faded as she demonstrated herself to be a masterful teacher. She won the love of her students and the respect of the administration. Ford went on to earn her bachelor's degree in 1966.

Ford and her husband separated in 1972, after which she moved with her daughter to Buffalo, New York. Ford wanted her daughter, nine-year-old Wynter Scott, to be close to her family who lived there.

It was around that time that her family and friends started seeing changes in her behavior. She was becoming delusional. She started reporting sightings of her husband and made claims that she had the soul of Jesus Christ. She also became an alcoholic.

In 1973, Ford and her daughter moved to Reno, Nevada. Life for her was becoming more difficult due to her delusions and drinking. She decided to seek help and admitted herself to the Nevada Mental Health Institute. After performing a mental evaluation, she was diagnosed as having a passive-aggressive personality with hysterical episodes. She stayed at the clinic to receive treatment and become stable again, after which she was released.

A stubborn woman, Ford did not keep up with her visits to the clinic and soon returned to drinking. Additionally, her delusions became more frequent. In 1974, she was arrested for trespassing, and her daughter was taken away by social workers. Her daughter was placed in Wittenberg Hall, a juvenile detention center located in Reno.

Having her daughter taken away from her put her over the edge. She had lost her husband and now, her daughter. Desperate, she moved back to New York. Because of her delusional thinking and her resistance to see a psychiatrist, her family would not take her in. She turned to Catholic charities for help. All she could think of was her daughter, who she believed was kidnapped by Reno authorities.

With the stress of not having her daughter and unwillingness to get treatment, she went on a quest to get her daughter back. Though her daughter was in Reno, she drove to Idaho in 1978. It was there that she did go to a mental health hospital for help. In 1979, she drove back to Buffalo, where she admitted herself as well. During her stay there, she was given a diagnosis of paranoid schizophrenia.

In May 1979, she moved to the state of Maine. She consulted with an attorney about getting her daughter back. The attorney explained that he could not help her, to which she replied, "I would drive across the state and kill everyone I saw along the way, and the people of Reno will pay in death."

The Thanksgiving Massacre

Feeling as though she has been abandoned, Ford decided she would return to Reno and try to get help there. She got a job wrapping packages at Macy's department store, hoping it would lead her to a better position within the store. Her goal was to raise enough money so she could retain a Nevada lawyer and get her daughter back.

On Thanksgiving Day, Ford became despondent. Her attempt to raise enough money seemed impossible. In her delusional thinking, she heard the voice of Joan Kennedy, the wife of Senator Edward Kennedy, telling her, "Just run through a whole bunch of people and kill everyone."

With a blood-alcohol level of .162, Ford got into her black 1974 Lincoln Continental and did exactly that.

She drove through town around 2:50 p.m. and reached the southeast corner of Virginia Street. It was busy with foot traffic as tourists and residents filled the sidewalk; a steady flow of people came and went through the many casinos. Ford hit the accelerator, and her Lincoln Continental jumped the curb and barreled down the sidewalk, traveling 100 feet.

Screams filled the air as her car plowed through the crowd, sending bodies flying. A woman was carried over 100 feet on her hood, before falling off. Ford got back on Virginia Street and drove until she reached the corner of Second Street. The traffic prevented her from going any further. It was there that she was arrested.

Sentencing

At her preliminary trial, she pleaded not guilty due to insanity. A judge ordered that she be sent to a psychiatric hospital until it was determined she could stand trial.

She was deemed competent to stand trial on August 4th, 1981. During her five-month trial, Priscilla Ford's defense attorney did not want her to testify, but she insisted on it. When she took the witness stand, she claimed to be Jesus Christ, and referred to the people that she killed as 'pigs.'

The jury found Ford guilty on March 19th, 1982, on six counts of murder and 23 counts of attempted murder.

She was sent to death row but died January 29th, 2005 from emphysema, at 75.

III
Adam Lanza

THE TEACHER TOLD HER FIFTH-GRADE CLASS that it was time for them to turn in their assignments. Her students were given the assignment to create their own comic book as part of a creative writing assignment. The comic book that one of the students turned in was called *"The Big Book of Granny."*

Intrigued by the title, she read it as her students exited class for recess. The teacher's intrigue turned to concern as she read the book that focused on the killing of children and cannibalism. It also discussed taxidermy. Though she found it upsetting, she did not express her concern to anyone. That teacher was just one of the many adults who did not notice the warning signs during the course of that child's life. That child was Adam Peter Lanza.

Challenge from Birth

Adam Lanza was born in Sandy Hook on April 22nd, 1992, a community within Newton, Connecticut. From the time he was born, his parents were concerned about the developmental challenges Lanza was exhibiting, particularly in the areas of language, motor skills, and sensory integration. He also demonstrated repetitive behaviors. He was eventually diagnosed as being on the autism spectrum, and having obsessive-compulsive disorder and anxiety.

His early years in elementary school seemed normal, but things changed when he started the fifth grade. He became increasingly fearful and avoided eye contact. Lanza attended Newton High School when he was 14. Though nervous, he was intelligent and made the 2007 honor roll. Despite his intellectual accomplishments, things went downhill for Lanza. He was always quiet, became even more withdrawn, and increasingly anxious. He was so anxious that in a 2004 incident, his mother had to bring him to the emergency room. By the time he turned 16, Lanza had missed most of the school year. His parents took him out of public school and homeschooled him.

Against the recommendations of the professionals who worked with Lanza, his mother made excuses for her son and accommodated his insecurities rather than challenging him to move beyond his comfort zone.

Lanza's Downward Spiral

Lanza did go back to school for the 10th grade, but his performance in school deteriorated. He became further withdrawn and had to complete his high school education through tutors, independent study, and attending classes at the community college.

When Lanza graduated from high school in 2009, his anxiety became so bad that he refused to leave his room. He covered up his windows and communicated with his mother through email. His parents had separated in 2002, at which time Lanza stopped all communication with his father.

Lanza became anorexic, weighing just 112 pounds at six feet. He rarely ate, eating only vegan when he did. Most of the time, he spent sleeping, which was the way he avoided his feelings of discomfort. Lanza separated himself from the rest of the world. He even avoided sunlight, saying that it hurts his eyes. There was one world that Lanza did feel safe in, and that was the online world.

Lanza was obsessed with mass murderers and spree killers. He admired the shooters of the 1999 Columbine High School attack, which resulted in the deaths of 12 students and a teacher. He developed a spreadsheet where he documented the details of all recorded cases of mass shootings. He would spend hours chatting with members of online groups who shared his interest.

Lanza felt alone, that he had no one whom he could depend on. He felt rejected by everyone. Lanza decided that he would join the ranks of his heroes Eric Harris and Dylan Klebold, the shooters of the Columbine massacre. A town of only 28,000 residents, Newton had only one murder over a 10-year period.

On December 14th, 2012, Lanza decided to change that.

The Sandy Hook Shooting

Before Lanza became a recluse, his mother, 52-year-old Nancy Lanza, often took him and his brother to the firing range. His mother was a gun-fanatic and owned over a dozen firearms.

In the early morning of December 14th, Lanza woke up and got dressed in all-black clothing and a green utility vest. He also grabbed a pair of sunglasses, yellow earplugs, and his mother's .22-caliber Savage MK 11-F bolt action rifle.

While she was sleeping, Lanza shot her four times in the head. He got into his mother's car and drove to Sandy Hook Elementary School.

The principal of Sandy Hook Elementary School, Dawn Hochsprung, started off her morning with a meeting that included the school's psychologist and other faculty members. During the meeting, they heard unusual sounds over the intercom system. What they did not know was those were the sounds of gunshots.

Hochsprung and the other faculty members stepped into the hallway to investigate the sounds, and they came face-to-face with Lanza. Hochsprung yelled, "Shooter! Stay put!", warning others.

Teachers grabbed any children in their proximity and herded them into classrooms. The school janitor, Rick Thorne, yelled at Lanza to put his gun down. Lanza shot him and then killed Hochsprung and Mary Sherlach. He also shot teacher Natalie Hammond, hitting her twice. She lay wounded on the floor. She acted as though she was dead until Lanza moved on toward the school's main office. That is when she crawled back to the conference room.

When Lanza saw that no one was in the main office, he resumed his patrol of the hallways. An eerie silence filled the air. It was disturbed only by the sound of gunshots. Some teachers and students hid from Lanza. The school nurse, Sarah Cox, took refuge under her desk. In other parts of the school, teachers and students stampeded toward the gymnasium for safety. As the chaos ramped up, the school's secretary, Barbra Halstead, called 911.

Lanza entered the classroom of Rachel D'Avino, who had sought safety there, along with 14 first-graders she'd managed to gather up. In a spray of gunfire, Lanza murdered them all. Lanza continued his reign of terror as he entered one classroom after another, shooting anybody he encountered.

With the arrival of the police, Lanza shot himself.

He had taken the life of 20 children and six adults in the school.

IV

Brenda Spencer

IN JULY OF 1979, THE IRISH ROCK BAND THE BOOM Town Rats, released their biggest hit, *"I Don't Like Mondays."* It became the #1 single in the United Kingdom. The song was inspired by a quote from a shooter, responsible for the 1979 mass killing at Grover Cleveland Elementary School.

It was the first mass shooting at a school within the United States.

The killer, Brenda Ann Spencer, was a 16-year-old, freckle-faced girl.

No Place for A Child

Spencer was born on April 3rd, 1962. She lived in San Carlos, a neighborhood of San Diego. Spencer's appearance made her the subject of mockery by other children as she was 5'2" tall, extremely thin, and had a head of bright red hair. Spencer had a natural talent for photography and won first prize in a competition.

Spencer's parents were divorced, and she and her older brother lived with her father, who was an alcoholic. Though the neighborhood they lived in was middle class, the conditions of their ranch-style home reflected a stark poverty and darkness. Their home was filthy and littered with empty beer cans and bottles from the father's drinking. There were just a few pieces of furniture, and the bed was a dirty old mattress on the floor, which she and her father shared.

With her unusual looks and grim living conditions, Spencer rarely engaged with other children, spending most of her time alone. She also self-identified as being gay. The darkness within her grew as she became further withdrawn. Spencer experienced difficulty in school as she did not feel comfortable there. She was placed in a special program for students with truancy issues. In

1978, she told a staff member she was feeling suicidal. She also started to torture cats.

During the summer of 1978, she was arrested for shooting at a school window of Grover Cleveland Elementary School with her B.B. gun. She was also accused of burglarizing the school. The school was located across the street from her house. Her probation officer arranged for her to have a psychiatric evaluation and for her to be admitted to a mental health hospital for observation, but her father refused to give his permission.

The Sin of The Father

On Christmas 1978, her father gave her a gift that would change the trajectory of her life and confirmed how her father really felt about her. She had asked her father for a radio, but when she opened her gift, it was a Ruger 10/22 semi-automatic .22 caliber rifle. Included were a telescopic sight and 500 rounds of ammunition.

The thought that came to her mind was that her father was hoping she would kill herself.

Spencer fell into despair. She envied other children who had someone in their life to protect them. She also resented them for the way they mocked her. She created a psychological cocoon for herself, where all human beings died.

On January 29th, 1979, at 8:30 a.m., Spencer grabbed the rifle, opened her bedroom window, and aimed it at Grover Cleveland Elementary.

The students of Grover Cleveland were arriving for class. They were being dropped off by their parents and lining up by the school's gate. 53-year-old Burton Wragg, the principal, was out greeting the children; while 56-year-old Michael Suchar, the school's custodian, was emptying a trash can into the dumpster.

A strange sense of satisfaction overtook Spencer as she pulled the trigger, sending a barrage of bullets to where the students were standing. The children screamed in terror as Wragg tried to lead the children to safety. The next bullet from Spencer's gun hit Wragg, seriously wounding him. Suchar tried to drag Wragg to safety when he was hit and killed. Wragg died shortly afterward.

The children, many of them injured, were brought into the cafeteria, and the school was placed on lockdown. The vice-principal contacted 911. A police officer, who was there for unrelated reasons, was shot in the neck when he attempted to assist.

Comments from Behind the Barricade

Spencer barricaded herself in her home. Her father and brother were not home at the time. A SWAT team arrived, and a police negotiator tried to persuade her to surrender. At one point during their conversation, Spencer told him that shooting at the children was 'easy pickings…like shooting ducks on a pond.' She also told him that she liked to watch the children squirm after they were hit.

A reporter managed to call her and asked her why she did it. She replied, "I don't like Mondays."

Spencer remained barricaded in the home for seven hours before surrendering to the police. During the assault, she got off 30 rounds of ammunition. Two people were killed and eight people were injured during the attack.

After her arrest, it was determined that she had an injury to the temporal lobe of the brain.

Sentencing

Spencer pled guilty to two counts of murder and assault with a deadly weapon. She was tried as an adult and sentenced to 25 years to life.

She is being held at the California Institution for Women in Chino, California.

Her request for parole has been denied several times. Her next request can be filed in 2021.

V

Jared Lee Loughner

IT WAS A SATURDAY MORNING, AND THE CLERK AT the Circle K Convenience Store watched the agitated young man as he paced before the store counter. He had come to the store to use their phone to call for a taxi. He had a lanky build and wore a hooded sweatshirt. Looking at the clock on the wall, he said out loud, "9:25. I still got time."

John Marion drove his taxi to the Circle K store on West Cortaro Farms Road. The 60-year-old man had been collecting fares and driving passengers on the streets of Tucson, Arizona for years. He pulled up to the curb and saw the clerk through the window of the Circle K store. She had one finger pointed up, letting him know that his passenger was on his way.

The young man got in the cab and asked him to take him to the Safeway Grocery Store on Oracle Road, on the Northwest side of Tucson. Their five-mile drive to the store was mostly silent, except for a few odd questions and comments. He asked Marion if he remembered all the people he picked up. The young man also told him that he drank too much. Other than that, he was quiet.

When they arrived at the Safeway store, the young man handed Marion a 20-dollar bill for a fare of $14.25. Marion did not have change as the young man was his first fare for the morning, which was January 8th, 2011. Rather than letting Marion have the 20-dollar bill, he asked him if he would go with him into the Safeway store to get change, which they did. The young man shook Marion's hand and thanked him, noticing the young man's hand was sweaty.

Marion left the store and returned to his cab. He noticed that workers were in the Safeway parking lot, setting up for an event to be held that day; a meet-and-greet with Arizona Representative Gabrielle Gifford.

Later that day, Marion would catch the breaking news as he sat on his couch. A shooter at the Gifford event had killed six people.

When a photograph of the gunman was broadcast, Marion recognized him. The killer had been his first fare from that morning, Jared Lee Loughner.

From Coltrane to Chaos

Loughner was born on September 10th, 1988, in Tucson, Arizona. He lived with his parents, Randy and Amy Loughner, on Soledad Avenue. It was a part of the Orangewood Estates Subdivision in northern Tucson. Amy was a doting mother to Loughner, who was her only child.

Loughner showed a love for the saxophone from early on, and she took him to music lessons and school concerts. He became a member of the Arizona Jazz Academy. His relationship with his father was the complete opposite. He never spoke of his dad with anyone. Randy Loughner was very private and standoffish. Jarred was uncomfortable being around him as were the neighbors, who saw him as being a scary character.

For Jarred, music was a form of escape as he delved into the musical world of Charlie Parker and John Coltrane. While attending Mountain View High School, he was active in music, playing the saxophone, drums, and writing music. He was also involved in creative writing and poetry. Those who knew Loughery saw him as an ordinary kid until he reached his senior year at Mountain View High School. It was then that a darkness overtook him.

The voices in his head took on a different quality. When he was younger, he could easily dismiss them, but not anymore. Frequently, his mother would walk past his room and hear him talking to himself. Others around him took notice of this as well. Friends and other students witnessed him making strange and disjointed comments. He stopped hanging around with friends and became isolated. He also started drinking and getting involved with drugs.

In the spring of 2006 when he was a senior, Loughery showed up to Mountain View drunk, having consumed almost an entire bottle of vodka early that morning. He was so intoxicated that he had to be hospitalized. His father had not been pleased and had yelled at him. Shortly after the incident, Loughery dropped out of high school.

He later enrolled at Pima Community College, where he took courses ranging from music fundamentals to computer logic. Pima College offered him the intellectual stimulation he desired.

Unfortunately, it was also the place where his behavior escalated and became even more erratic. This created concern campus-wide.

In February, the campus police were called to the classroom because Loughner was on a tirade during a class discussion. Students were discussing the poem of another student when Jerrod disrupted the class by loudly explaining his interpretation of the poem, which had no relevance to the context of the poem. He excitedly talked about abortion, war, and the killing of people.

In April, the school's library had to call the police because Loughner refused to stop making bizarre noises while he was listening to music. In May, Loughner's Pilates instructor called the campus police out of fear for her safety. Loughner exploded in anger when he received a 'B' in her course. In June, he disrupted his math class by arguing with the instructor, who had referred to the number '6' as 'six' when Loughner insisted that he refer to the number as 'eighteen.'

Loughner was paranoid about authority figures and obsessed with conspiracy theories. His favorite books were *Animal Farm*, *Fahrenheit 451*, *Mein Kampf*, and *The Communist Manifesto*. His extreme anti-government and anti-authoritarian political stance became well-known on campus. He believed that the September 11 attacks on the Twin Towers were the work of the United States government and that the banking system was creating slaves out of the American people. He had a deep hatred for President George W. Bush.

The Merchant of Fear

An active user of YouTube, he frequently shared his beliefs. He released a video titled, "Pima Community College School-Genocide," where he accused the school of torturing students.

His bizarre behavior led to a genuine fear among the students, the faculty, and the community.

Some students and teachers believed that Loughner would one day bring a gun to school. Female tellers at a nearby bank feared for their safety whenever he came around. He would sternly tell them they should not be working there and should not be in a position of power. They found his physical appearance alone scary as he had shaved his head and eyebrows.

The university system had had it with Loughner. University administrators notified him that he would no longer be permitted to attend any of their classes.

Loughner decided to return to the military. He went to the recruiting office and underwent an interview.

During the interview, he told the recruiter that he took drugs. The recruiter refused his application. Upon getting the results of his drug test, the recruiting office discovered that the results of his test showed him to be clean. Loughner faced rejection from both Pima College and the military. He was also fired by his previous employer, the Pima Animal Control Center, where he volunteered because he could not follow instructions.

The Unanswered Question

Loughner became a recluse and stayed in his room. He was watching the news when they announced that U.S. Representative Gabrielle Gifford, a Democrat, would be holding a meet and greet in his area. He felt a sense of anger as he listened to the announcement.

He remembered when he attended one of her speaking engagements in 2007. Gifford had been holding her annual "Congress in Your Corner." He had asked Gifford the following question, "What is government if words have no meaning?" Gifford declined to answer his question. Loughner felt anger.

Loughner's parents were concerned about their son's mental stability and feared he might hurt himself or someone else. His father came up with a way to alter his son's car so he could not drive it. Unfortunately, he neglected to do so on the morning of January 8th, 2011.

Early that morning, Loughner got in his car and drove off to a sporting goods store to buy ammunition, the same store where he had bought a Glock two months earlier.

Loughner purchased a 33-round magazine and placed it in his backpack. When he got home, his father questioned him about what he had in his backpack. Loughner ran out of the house and headed to the desert.

When he thought his dad was no longer a threat to his plan, Loughner walked toward the Circle K store to call for a cab. When the cab dropped him off at the Safeway Grocery Store, Loughner hung around until Gabriella Gifford's meet and greet started.

The event started, and those who were in attendance burst out in applause as Gifford took the stage. Accompanying her was her 30-year-old congressional aide, Gabriel M. Zimmerman, and 63-year-old district judge John M. Rolls. Loughner got out of his seat as Gifford took the microphone.

As Loughner raised his gun, he had memories of the last time she had refused to answer his question. Gifford was the first one to get hit as Loughner shot at the stage and into the crowd. Zimmerman and Roll were shot as well as members of the audience, including 76-year-old Dorothy J. Morris, 76-year-old Dorwan C. Stoddard, 79-year-old Phyllis C. Schneck, and nine-year-old Christina–Taylor Green.

Deputy Sheriff Thomas Audetat and two civilians rushed Loughner and knocked him to the ground. They restrained him until back-up could arrive. In the course of the attack, Loughner had shot off 31 rounds in the 19-second attack. Six people were killed, including Green and Rolls. 14 people were wounded, including Gifford, who was shot at close range. Her injuries left her with impaired speech and vision, and paralysis of her right arm and leg.

Sentencing

Loughner pleaded not guilty to multiple charges of murder and attempted murder.

A psychiatric evaluation showed that he had schizophrenia and was incompetent to stand trial. He was sent to a federal psychiatric facility in Missouri, where he received treatment.

He was eventually deemed competent to agree to a plea deal, which made him ineligible for parole or to appeal his conviction. He was sentenced to 140 years in prison.

VI

Seung Hui Cho

THE CO-DIRECTOR OF THE CREATIVE WRITING program, Lucinda Roy, was in her office at Virginia Tech. She was talking to a colleague about the concerns she had for one of her students. She stated that the student was the loneliest person she had ever met. She explained how this student always wore sunglasses while in class, wore a baseball cap pulled low over his eyes, and spoke in a whisper. He also had the odd habit of taking pictures during class time with his cell phone. She also felt unsafe around him. That student was Seung Hui Cho.

The teacher had a right to be concerned as he would soon be known as the shooter in the Virginia Tech Massacre.

Sullen and Silent

Hui Cho was born on January 18th, 1984, in South Korea. He and his family came to the United States in 1992. They first went to Detroit before moving to Centreville, Virginia, where his parents worked in dry cleaning. From the time he was born, his parents were concerned about Hui Cho's temperament. Besides being very quiet and shy, he always had a sullen expression on his face. He did not interact with other children.

Hui Cho attended Westfield High School in Fairfax County and graduated in 2003. Throughout his high school years, he continued to be a loner. Hui Cho rarely engaged with his teachers or other students. He rarely spoke.

Jelly and Other Madness

From high school, Hui Cho enrolled at Virginia Tech. It was there that his behavior took a dramatic turn. He had a roommate with whom he occasionally communicated. One day, he told his roommate that he had a girlfriend that was a supermodel and she lived in outer space. He called her Jelly. At the end of the day, his roommate returned to the dorm, at Harper Hall, when Hui Cho told him that he needed to go elsewhere as he wanted to be alone with Jelly.

His preoccupation with Jelly faded when he turned his attention onto female classmates. Hui Cho would constantly send them Instant Messages and show up in their dorm room. Despite his female classmates filing complaints against Hui Cho, he persisted in this behavior. It got so bad that the two students stopped coming to class. Campus authorities ordered him to stop in December 2005, which led him to tell his roommate he was going to commit suicide.

A counselor familiar with Hui Cho advised that he be involuntarily committed to a mental hospital. A judge agreed, citing him as a danger, and he was sent to Carilion St. Albans Psychiatric Hospital. The psychiatrist concluded that Hui Cho was mentally ill but not a threat to others, so the judge ordered him to seek outpatient treatment.

Pushed Too Far

For Hui Cho, each day that passed while attending Virginia Tech, continued to remind him just how alone he was. He felt the world was out to get him. Virginia Tech, its instructors, administrators, counselors, and other students were all after him. His hatred grew, and his sense of kinship with the mass shooters he read about had deepened. He knew what he had to do; he had to fight back. The world had pushed him too far. It was time to take action.

On March 13th, he purchased a Glock 9-mm handgun. On March 31st, Hui Cho went to Walmart, where he purchased the items from a list that he had made the night before. He returned to that Walmart on April 7th and 8th, with a final trip on April 13th. Over that time period, he bought ammunition, a pair of cargo pants, gloves, a hunting knife, and a granola bar. He also went to Dick's Sporting Goods, where he bought additional magazines of ammunition. Sometime after April 13th, he also purchased a Walther .22 caliber pistol.

With his cache of weapons and supplies fully stocked, he got a room at a nearby motel where he would stay until April 16th. For the final steps of his preparation, he went for a haircut. He requested a military buzz cut. He then had an intense workout at his gym.

On April 16th, 2007, Hui Cho left his motel room and headed for Virginia Tech. His rampage began at 7:00 a.m., when he entered West Ambler Johnston Hall. The dorm was largely empty, but he saw two students in the commons area. Caught by surprise, they had no time to react. Hui Cho shot them both, killing them instantly. Other students, who were in the dormitory, heard the shots and were able to escape through another entrance.

Hui Cho left the building and entered Harper Hall, which was next to a post office. He mailed a package to NBC News that contained some of his writings and video recordings. Hui Cho then proceeded to Norris Hall, where he, without a hint of emotion on his face, started firing at anyone he saw. Students and staff members screamed as they fled for their lives across hallway floors stained red by the blood of those who did not make it.

Hui Cho then entered a classroom, which he sprayed with bullets. The instructor died instantly, as did many of the students. Their bullet-ridden bodies lay slumped in their chairs. In other classrooms, students and instructors were barricading the doorways or running for the exits as Hui Cho continued his rampage.

When the police arrived, Hui Cho shot himself in the head.

In the end, 30 people were killed and 17 were injured.

VII
Charles Joseph Whitman

ON AUGUST 1ST, 1966, AUSTIN POLICE WERE called to the apartment of Margaret Whitman by a caller who had heard a gunshot coming from the apartment. When the police entered the Texan woman's home, they found her dead from a gunshot wound and multiple stabbings. Beside her was a note, "Truly sorry that this was the only way I could see to relieve her sufferings, but I think it was best."

Within hours, another call was made to the Austin Police, reporting a disturbance coming from the home of Charles Whitman. In the home, they found the body of Kathryn Whitman. She was in her bed and had been stabbed to death. Beside her body, there was also a note, this one stating, "I love her dearly...I cannot rationally pinpoint any specific reason for doing this."

Austin authorities would later find out that these two murders were just the beginning, for by the end of the day, they would get to know the devastating destruction of Charles Whitman.

From Altar Boy to Madness

Whitman was born on June 24th, 1941, in the city of Lake Worth, Florida. The family lived on South L Street in a home that no one felt safe in. His father, Charles Adolphus Whitman Jr., was a perfectionist who was very demanding of his family. He also had a violent temper and was physically abusive toward his wife Margaret and their children.

Whitman did his best to please his father and pushed himself to win his acceptance. The older of three children, Whitman took piano lessons at age 5. By age 6, he scored 138 on an IQ test. When he turned 12, he became an Eagle Scout. He also was an altar boy.

When he turned 18, he joined the Marines. Whitman went through boot camp in South Carolina, where he achieved the status of a sharpshooter. He did a year's service at Guantanamo Navy Base. In September of 1961, Whitman attended the University of

Texas where he studied mechanical engineering. His education was made possible through military scholarship.

Whitman tried to keep himself on track; however, he could only run from his past for so long. The fear, anger, and resentment he felt as a child could no longer be contained. The evil inflicted by his father reared its ugly head within him. Like his father, he had tried to deny his past. Like his father, his past could no longer be suppressed. His inner darkness started to leak out and take over his life.

In 1963, Whitman killed a deer and brought it back to his dormitory. He hung the deer in the shower and skinned it. The incident, along with his slipping grades, resulted in his scholarship being revoked. Because he lost his scholarship, he decided to go back to the Marines.

He started to behave erratically in the military, gambling and having a firearm on base. He also threatened another Marine over a loan that was past due. Military superiors discovered that the loan to the other Marine had been for $30, and Whitman was charging him 50% interest. As a result of his behavior, he was court-martialed. His punishment was a month of confinement, three months of hard labor, and demotion to the rank of Private.

Whitman received an honorable discharge in December 1964. He decided to return to the University of Texas and study architectural engineering. As he was without a scholarship, he worked as a bill collector and a bank teller.

In 1966, Whitman learned that his mother was leaving his father. Fed up with his abuse, she moved to Austin, where she found an apartment. His father would continuously call him, begging him to convince his mother to return to him. Whitman refused his father's requests.

With all the pressures he was experiencing, Whitman fell into a depression. He talked to the university's doctor, who prescribed him Valium. He was also advised that he should see the university's psychiatrist. Whitman did see the psychiatrist and shared with her the frustrations he was experiencing over his parent's divorce, as well as the stress from work and school. At some point during the session, Whitman told her, in a fit of anger, of his desire to just "start shooting people with a deer rifle" from the University tower. The psychiatrist recommended he return for another session. That never happened.

The Tower

On August 1st, 1966, Whitman woke up with a pounding headache and a feeling of despair. He saw no future in his life. His feeling of loneliness cut deep to his core. He decided it was time to get back at all those who had done him wrong. He left his apartment and drove to town; he was preparing for war.

Whitman's first stop was at the Austin Rental Company where he rented a dolly. From there, he went to the bank and cashed a $250 check. With money in hand, he purchased an M1 Carbine and a 12-gauge shotgun. When he returned home, he gathered other things he would need: 6-mm Remington rifle, .357 Magnum, Galesi-Brescia pistol, Luger pistol, a machete, ammunition, knives, a radio, binoculars, canteen, alarm clock, rope, gloves, food, and water.

He sawed off the shotgun barrel and changed clothes, dressing in khaki coveralls and a green jacket. After packing his cache of weapons and supplies into wooden crates, he loaded up his truck and drove off. His destination was the University of Texas.

He made two stops on the way. He killed his mother. He killed his wife.

He headed to the university. Upon arriving on campus, he drove up to the security gate and presented his badge, which he had retained from the time he had been a research assistant at the university. He told security he was making a delivery. Security provided him with a parking pass.

The Main building, also known as the "Tower," was located in the center of the University of Texas campus. Standing at 307 feet, the Tower has 30 floors. At 11:30 a.m., Whitman pushed his dolly of supplies into the main building and headed for the elevator. He pushed the elevator button, but nothing happened. An employee advised Whitman the power to the elevator was off, but turned it on for him. Thanking the employee, Whitman entered the elevator and headed for the top floor.

As the elevator traveled to the top, he continued to strategize how the operation would unfold. When he reached the top floor, he headed to the observation deck. With the iconic clock face above him, he started to unload the crates when he spotted Edna Townsley, a receptionist at the building. He hit her over the head with the butt of his rifle, causing her to lose consciousness. He hid her body; she would later die from her injuries. He also spotted a young couple admiring the view from the tower.

When the couple left the observation deck, he barricaded the stairwell. A few minutes later, two families, who had climbed up the stairs, were trying to look over the barricade. The families were tourists and had wanted to see the view from the observation deck. Whitman took out his rifle and shot them. Two family members were killed while a third one suffered permanent disabilities.

Whitman unpacked all his weapons and was ready. He started shooting from the tower. His targets were anyone he saw on the campus below him. One of his first victims was a 17-year-old boy riding a bicycle. His bullet went through the boy's groin. An 18-year-old pregnant woman, Claire Wilson, and her companion, Thomas Eckman, were walking across the campus mall when both were hit. Only Claire survived. Her baby and her companion were killed instantly.

Robert Boyer, a researcher and lecturer, was shot in the back when he was leaving the main building. A chemistry student, Abdul Khashab, and his fiancée, Janet Paulos, were both wounded, as was Lana Phillips, who was in their company. In an adjacent building, a shop manager received a bullet in the leg when Whitman fired into the store window. Harry Walchuk, a political science graduate student, was fatally wounded when a bullet hit him in the throat.

Claudia Rutt and 18-year-old Paul Sonntag were both gunned down as they were taking a stroll. 17-year-old Karen Griffith was mortally wounded when she was shot in the chest.

When the gunfire first started, Michael Hall, who worked in the history department, contacted the police. He advised them that he had heard a gunshot, and people were wounded.

Over 100 law enforcement officers convened on the university; they included members from the Texas Rangers, police officers, highway patrolmen, and secret service men from the Austin office of Lyndon B. Johnson. They had never encountered a mass shooting like the one they were witnessing. Not only was it their first mass shooting, but they also could not tell the exact location of the gunman.

Eventually, an off-duty patrol officer, Ramiro Martinez, with the help of another officer and a small group of private citizens, made their way up the tower and fatally shot Whitman.

The two-hour rampage took the lives of 14 innocent people and left 30 wounded.

During his autopsy, it was discovered that Whitman had a brain tumor.

VIII

Mark Barton

IT WAS ON CHRISTMAS DAY, 1998, WHEN 27-YEAR-old Leigh Ann Barton first heard of her estranged husband's trouble. 43-year-old Mark Barton told her that he had lost a fortune in the stock market. A day trader, Mark told her, "'I lost it all. I need help."

What she could not know was that she would join 12 people who would lose their lives during her estranged husband's killing spree.

His killing spree would begin in her own home and continue at his trading firm, where his last words would be, "I hope this doesn't ruin your trading day."

Moving on Up

Standing at 6'4", dark-haired, and tanned, Barton would seem to have it all. Besides being handsome, he worked for two trading firms: Momentum Securities brokerage and All-Tech Investment Group. Both firms are located in Two Securities Centre Building, a part of Atlanta's upscale district.

He had come a long way to get where he was. Born April 2nd, 1955 to military parents, Barton was an only child. His previous life was that of a manual laborer until he attended community college in Georgia. While in college, he drifted without any sense of direction. Realizing that he needed to make a change, he eventually enrolled at the University of Southern Carolina. While attending school, Barton worked as a night auditor at a hotel; it was there where he met Debra Spivey, who also attended USC.

Barton graduated in 1979 with a degree in chemistry and found a job testing cleaning chemicals. During the same year, he also married Spivey. The couple then moved to Texarkana, Texas, where he eventually became the president of TLC Manufacturing Company, which he and some of his friends had founded.

True Colors

Though he became president of the company in 1988, he parted ways with the company in 1990. Mysteriously, the day after he quit, someone broke into the company's office and stole propriety formulas and erased computer files. Detectives went to his home to question him about the break-in. On that same day, they received a call from TLC to drop the case against Barton, citing the company had reached an agreement with Barton. Detectives suspected the intentions of the break-in were not to steal anything; instead, it was to hide evidence of kickbacks, inventory discrepancies, and possible illegal drug activity.

Barton and his wife moved back to Georgia, where he found a sales position with a chemical company. It was then that he found himself attracted to the company's receptionist, Leigh Ann Lang. Barton's marriage was on the rocks and Lang was a welcome distraction.

In 1993, Spivey had plans to visit her mother in Alabama for Labor Day. Just before she left, Barton took out a $600,000 life insurance policy on her.

On the last day of the Labor Day weekend, the police in Alabama contacted him to advise that both his wife and her mother were found butchered in her mother's trailer. Their bodies had been hacked-up by the killer, who detectives believed used an ax.

In the same month of the killings, Barton and Lang began their romance, and Barton was buying a new wardrobe and frequenting tanning salons. They got married on May 26, 1995, less than two years after the killings. In June 1995, Barton and his new wife moved to the city of Stockbridge, where they found an apartment.

The happiness and passion that the two shared did not last. Lang became unhappy in the marriage and would often leave him. Things became even more difficult when Barton's two and half-year-old daughter, Mychelle, made serious allegations against her father. Mychelle, who Barton had while married to Spivey, told a day-care worker that Barton had molested her.

Though authorities suspected Barton of murdering Spivey and her mother, they could never prove it. When Barton underwent a mental evaluation due to his daughter's allegations of molesting her, the psychologist concluded that Barton was quite capable of committing murder. Because of Mychelle's age and the lack of any corroborating evidence, there was nothing that the district attorney could have done to separate Mychelle from her father.

Besides having Mychelle with Spivey, Barton also had a son with her named Matthew. Both Mychelle and Matthew were an important factor in a trial that Barton was facing. After Spivey's death, Barton almost immediately tried to collect the insurance money. The insurance company challenged Barton's request by bringing him to court. Like many others, they, too, suspected that Barton played a role in the deaths of Spivey and her mother.

During the 1997 trial, lawyers for the insurance company were concerned that the jury would sympathize with Mychelle and Matthew. The insurance company decided to settle the case by awarding Barton $450,000 with the stipulation that $150,000 goes to a trust for the children's education. With the financial settlement, Barton entered the world of day trading.

Barton became a full-time day-trader at Momentum Securities and All-Tech Investment Group. He dealt with volatile internet stocks. By June of 1997, Barton had lost $105,000. Eventually, both financial firms closed his accounts as he was unable to put up the needed cash to cover his debt. Barton deposited $50,000 to reopen the account, but it bounced.

An Investment into Terror

On July 29, 1999, Barton walked into the office of All-Tech Investment Group. That same day, the Dow Jones fell by almost 200 points. Barton had lost all his money; he was also armed with two guns: a 9-mm Glock and a .45 caliber Colt. Barton fired five shots, wounding the manager and his assistant. He then moved on toward the main trading floor. He saw 53-year-old Nell Jones behind her computer. He fired at her but missed. He continued shooting across the trading floor.

Throughout the shooting, he did not say a word until he exited the building. That is when he uttered, "I hope this won't ruin your trading day." Barton then proceeded toward Momentum Securities, where mayhem continued.

When the police arrived at the building, they found a thick trail of blood in the hallway. As they searched the building, they found people hiding in closets, while others had thrown their computers out the windows to attract attention. In another room, five employees were slumped over their computers. Police searched the building but were unable to locate Barton. The officers posted outside the building, however, were able to gather information about Barton.

A group of employees, who were outside the building during the shooting, told the police that they saw a man who fit Barton's description, taking off on foot. He was running southbound toward the Buckhead Loop intersection. Another man saw the suspect running toward Phipps Plaza.

Officers, armed with shotguns and police dogs, searched the area as offices and schools went on lockdown. After a four-hour search, police got a tip that Barton was hiding in an unoccupied van parked at the Town Center Mall.

Police received a radio dispatch that Barton was driving the van on Interstate 75. Cobb County Officer Huel Clements, who was patrolling Interstate 75, spotted the van. Clements followed the van, taking care not to be spotted by Barton. At 7:50 p.m., Clements observed Barton turning off the interstate on to Georgia 92, in Acworth. Barton pulled into a BP gas station. Clements turned on his siren and lights. He accelerated into the gas station and positioned himself in front of the minivan. He jumped out of his patrol car and took cover behind the open door of the squad car. With his gun drawn, he ordered Barton out of the van.

While sitting in the van, Barton raised the two guns to his head and shot himself.

When detectives searched Barton's home, they discovered another shocking scene. Barton's wife and children were murdered. They had been pummeled by blows from a hammer.

In the room, they discovered a note written by Barton. It read, "I killed Leigh Ann because she was one of the main reasons for my demise... I know that Jehovah will take care of all of them in the next life. I'm sure the details don't matter. There is no excuse, no good reason I am sure no one will understand. If they could, I wouldn't want them to. I just write these things to say why. Please know that I love Leigh Ann, Matthew, and Mychelle with all my heart. If Jehovah's willing, I would like to see them all again in the resurrection to have a second chance. I don't plan to live very much longer, just long enough to kill as many of the people that greedily sought my destruction."

Barton had killed them on the 28th, the day before his rampage at the trading offices.

Including himself, Barton took 13 lives and wounded 13 others.

IX

Jennifer San Marco

DARLENE HAYES STEPPED OUTSIDE THE CIBOLA Counseling Services to head to her car and retrieve a notebook she had forgotten to take with her. Hayes was the manager of the counseling center which was located in Cibola, a county in New Mexico.

While she was in the parking lot, she saw 44-year-old Jennifer San Marco kneeling on the ground before the front tire of her car. Hayes thought she might have had a flat and walked over to assist. As she came closer, she heard San Marco talking to herself. Hayes asked her if anything was wrong, to which San Marcos replied, "They pray before they get in."

Puzzled by San Marco's remarks, Hayes asked her for clarification. San Marcos told her that she was referring to her brother and sister, of whom she said were with her.

Concerned for her safety, Hayes called the police, hoping they would help her get a mental health evaluation for San Marco. Hayes was concerned, believing that San Marco needed psychological attention immediately. After waiting for a period of time for the police to arrive, Hayes left. Hayes later learned that the police claimed to have never received her call to them. Had they responded, they might have been able to prevent one of the few spree killings perpetrated by a woman.

Singing Her Way into Madness

San Marco was born on December 6th, 1961, in New York. She attended Edward R. Murrow High School in Brooklyn, and went on to Brooklyn College. She later attended Rutgers University, where she studied natural resource management. San Marco dropped out of Rutgers and decided to move to California in 1989. She had worked at the Chuckawalla Valley State Prison as a security guard, but quit her job after a few months.

She then moved to the coastal city of Santa Barbara. She got a job at the sheriff's department as a police dispatcher. To be accepted for the position, she underwent an extensive background check and psychological evaluation. San Marco worked there for a few months before resigning.

In 1997, she started working the night shift at Goleta's Santa Barbara Processing and Distribution Center. A suburb of Santa Barbara County, Goleta offered a small-town atmosphere with proximity to the Pacific coast. The 200,000 square-foot processing center was near the University of Santa Barbara. San Marco liked the area enough to buy a condominium. In the year 2000, she took a second job where she served lunches at a nearby high school but quit after less than a year. It was around that time that an undiagnosed mental disorder began to take over her life.

San Marco's neighbor, 54-year-old Barbara Graham, was becoming irate with her. Graham chose to live in Goleta because she loved that it was a quiet community; however, San Marco changed that for her. San Marco would sing loudly outside, which frequently led to arguments between the two women. Her behavior became increasingly erratic as she began a pattern of shouting and cursing at empty air. She would also order food at restaurants and rush out the door before it was brought to her. Other times, she would kneel and pray on the street as well as take off her clothes in public.

Her bizarre behavior extended to the workplace. She would yell and curse at herself and other employees, especially minorities. She would go on racist rants, and her co-workers became scared of her. In 2003, her erratic behavior at work got so bad that they had to call the police, who escorted her out of the building. She was sent to Ventura Psychiatric Hospital for an assessment. She was also put on medical disability.

Convinced that the post office and the government were out to get her, San Marco sold her condominium and went to New Mexico in 2004. She spent time in Milan, a rural area 70 miles west of Albuquerque. She continued her aggressive behavior while she lived there. She would frequently go to the Milan Village Office to apply for permits for businesses she wanted to start, including pet food, and a publication titled, "The Racist Press." She would harass employees, especially minority employees. There was one employee she fixated on and would just stare at her.

Pay Back

In August 2005, San Marco purchased a 15-round, 9-mm Smith & Wesson Model 915 at Ace Pawn & Antiques. Despite her mental history, she passed the required background check.

On January 30th, 2006, San Marco traveled back to Santa Barbara, where she went to the home of her former neighbor, Beverly Graham, and shot her. She then drove to the Santa Barbara Processing and Distribution Center, arriving there at approximately 9:00 p.m. Despite the center's security, she was able to get in. She drove through the electronic gate by following the vehicle ahead of her. Once inside, she threatened an employee at gunpoint. She demanded their security pass, which allowed her to enter the building.

Once inside the building, San Marco started shooting, killing seven employees before she killed herself. All the victims were minorities.

X
Michael Kenneth McLendon

THE FLAMES ENGULFED THE HOUSE AND LIT UP the Alabama night. The residence was in the small town of Kinston, and the plight of the burning structure had escaped notice by any of the town's residents. As the home burned to the ground, a shadowy figure ran to a car parked in front of the house. The car sped off into the night; its driver was Michael Kenneth McLendon.

The burning house was his mother's home.

The terror that the small town was about to face had only just begun.

Living on A Dead-End Street

McLendon was born on September 19th, 1980, in Alabama. His parents divorced while he was very young. He was raised by his aunt and maternal uncle. McLendon was a bright child and an A-student while in high school. He graduated in 1999.

McLendon lived in Southern Alabama, which was hit hard when the country went through the worst economy since the Great Depression. Finding a job in Alabama's depressed economy was difficult. Many of the textile jobs were sent overseas. To make ends meet, he moved in with his mother in Kinston, a town in Coffee County. Kinston had a population of fewer than 540 people.

McLendon had always wanted to become a police officer. He applied to the Samson Police Department and was accepted to attend their police academy; however, he was unable to handle the training. McLendon dropped out of the academy after two weeks. He went on to find a job at Reliable Products in Geneva. He worked in the warehouse. He was let go from his job in 2003.

McLendon grew increasingly frustrated. He could not make it in his dream job as a police officer. His work history consisted of low-skilled jobs, which he never stayed for long. He also tried to join the Marines but was unsuccessful. He was 28, living with his mother, had limited skills, and only have a high school education. His choices were not plentiful.

He and his mother eventually got jobs working for Pilgrim Foods, a poultry processing plant. Their employment was suspended in 2006. They, along with other workers, filed a lawsuit against the company involving compensation.

McLendon's last job was working for Kelley Foods, a factory that produced sausage. His position was team leader, and he was well-liked by his co-workers. Despite this, McLendon was unhappy. He felt like a failure as he wanted a career. Instead, he felt that he was condemned to live a life where he worked menial jobs for minimum wage. He was further upset that his mother was not being supported by the family. As for his father, he had disappeared from his life long ago.

The one thing that gave him a sense of significance was his guns. He had been collecting them for years and had assembled a cache of weapons. He had been storing them in his mother's home without her being aware of it. He had assault rifles: Soviet SKS, a Bushmaster, and a 38-caliber pistol. He also had been amassing a large quantity of ammunition.

Deadly Family Matters

McLendon became depressed and began fantasizing about how he would strike back against those who were keeping him down. His fantasies became obsessive and gave him a sense of strength in a world where he felt helpless. Eventually, he stopped fantasizing and started developing a plan. That plan was implemented on March 10th, 2009.

While his mother was sleeping, McLendon shot her in the head. He also shot her three dogs and piled their corpses on top of her. He then got a pile of clothes and covered the dead bodies with them. He poured gasoline on the pile, lit a match, and ran out of the house.

McClendon got in his car, which contained his weapons and ammunition, and drove off toward the town of Samson, shooting anybody he saw along the way.

When he reached Samson, he drove by his uncle's home. James Alford White, 55 years old, was sitting on his porch when McLendon shot him, killing him instantly. A few houses down was the home of his cousin, 34-year-old Tracy Michelle Wise, who was the daughter of White. McLendon killed her with a single shot.

McLendon continued driving down the block and shot his second cousin, 15-year-old Dean James Wise, and their neighbor, 31-year-old Andrea Dawn Myers. Myers was the wife of Geneva County Sheriff Josh Myers. When he shot Myers, he also shot her child, 18-month-old Corinne Gracy Myers. McLendon reached the last house on the block, the home of his grandmother, 74-year-old Virginia E. White. McLendon fatally shot her as she stood in the doorway of her house.

The Chase

McLendon continued driving. When he saw a pedestrian walking along Wise Street, McClendon shot him dead and continued driving. Heading for the town of Geneva, McLendon passed the Inland store. Sonja Lolley Smith, 43 years old, was shopping there when she was shot. McLendon's final victim was a motorist that had passed him as he headed toward Samson.

McLendon was traveling on Highway 52, making his way toward Geneva. As he passed a Walmart, he fired shots into the store's window. A state trooper witnessed the shooting and pursued McClendon. The state trooper called for reinforcements as McLendon led him on a high-speed chase. Despite their speeds, McLendon managed to fire seven shots at the pursuing patrol car.

The state trooper was hit in the shoulder, suffering only minor injuries. McLendon sped off.

As he approached Reliable Metal Products, McLendon saw another police car pursuing him. The officer was Frankie Lindsey of the Geneva Police. McLendon refused to pull over.

When McLendon reached Reliable Metals, he got out of his car, ran into a building, and shot himself in the head.

During his murderous spree, McLendon killed 11 people and wounded six.

XI

Christopher Harper-Mercer

Laurel Mercer went to her neighbor's apartment and complained that her children were playing too loud. She went to another neighbor and complained about their barking dog. She then went from door to door, requesting her neighbors to sign a petition which called for the manager of the apartment complex to spray her apartment for cockroaches. The reason for these requests: her son. His fear of everything.

Her son, Christopher Harper-Mercer, who would later commit the worst mass shooting in Oregon's history.

Mother and Son

Christopher's father was Ian Mercer, who was from Lancashire, England. Ian Mercer moved to the U.S. to be with Laurel Harper, Christopher's mother. The couple lived in a small one-bedroom apartment in Torrance, California, where Christopher was born. The couple eventually separated.

Harper-Mercer spent most of his time with his mother, rarely leaving her side. Neighbors rarely saw them as they spent most of their time in their apartment. Harper-Mercer, quiet and shy, avoided encounters with others and barely spoke when others tried to converse with him. He attended the Switzer Center, a non-profit school that provided special education to students with learning disabilities, including Autism and Asperger's Syndrome.

While Harper-Mercer rarely talked, he transformed when the topic came to guns. His love for guns eventually led him to join the United States Army in 2008. He attended basic training in Fort Jackson, South Carolina. However, he was dismissed in less than five weeks for not meeting their minimum standards.

Strange Interests

Harper-Mercer and his mother moved to Winchester, Oregon, in 2013, for employment reasons. They rented an apartment. They had 14 firearms, all of which were legally purchased. Among their weapons were a Glock pistol and an AR-15 rifle with full magazines. Mother and son would frequently go to the firing range, one of the few places that Harper-Mercer felt comfortable.

In his reclusive existence, Harper-Mercer spent a lot of time online. He frequented message boards, where he posted comments about his anti-government and anti-religion stance. He also shared his pain of never having had a girlfriend. Most of all, he was fascinated with shootings and the gunmen that perpetuated them.

On August 31st, he expressed his sympathy for Vester Lee Flanagan II, the reporter who gunned down two of his colleagues while broadcasting live in Roanoke, Virginia. He posted the following comment, "I have noticed that people like him are all alone and unknown, yet when they spill a little blood, the whole world knows who they are, and seems the more people you kill, the more you're in the limelight."

He also admired Ted Bundy, Adam Lanza, as well as the Columbine shooters Eric Harris and Dylan Klebold. He admired them because, like him, they were rejected by society but struck back with a vengeance. He also had an affinity for the IRA, an Irish paramilitary group that engaged in a violent campaign aimed at gaining independence from Great Britain. To achieve their ends, they launched terrorist attacks, including an attempt to assassinate the British Prime Minister in 1984.

Breaking Point

Harper-Mercer enrolled at Umpqua Community College. He got involved in the Theater and Arts Department as well as taking a writing composition class. On September 1st, he received a notice that his grade point average was below a C, and that he would be suspended unless he raised it. He also received a tuition bill for $2,021 that was due on October 6th. He felt stressed out and began thinking of his mass shooting heroes.

On October 1st, 2015, around 10:30 a.m., Harper-Mercer arrived at Umpqua. He was armed with five handguns and one semi-automatic rifle. He entered his writing class and fired a single shot. He ordered his terrified instructor and classmates to gather in the center of the room. With a gun in each hand, he first shot his

English professor at close range as his students watched in terror. He then walked around the students, asking some of them what religious faith they belonged to. Those who affirmed their faith were shot in the head, while those who proclaimed no religious affiliation were shot in the leg.

Harper-Mercer then walked through the school, shooting at anyone he saw. One woman, who was retreating inside a classroom, was shot in the abdomen as she was closing the door. He encountered another woman and made her beg for her life; he shot her as well as another woman, who pleaded with him not to shoot the woman. He entered one classroom and saw a teacher taking refuge under her desk; he shot her in the leg. A handicapped girl was hiding in a corner; her wheelchair was across from her. He ordered her to get in her wheelchair. When she struggled to get to it, he shot her.

At 10:44 a.m., detectives from the Roseburg Police Department arrived at Snyder Hall. Harper-Mercer shot at them. The detectives returned fire and wounded him on the right side.

He took off to a classroom. He fired a bullet to his brains.

During the massacre, 10 people lost their lives, and another eight were injured.

XII

Dana Ewell

IT WAS THE DAY AFTER EASTER, AND ROSA AVITIA arrived at the Ewell's home in Sunnyside. Avitia had been their maid for years, and she felt like a member of the family. Sunnyside is a California town located near Fresno.

With a population of 4,000, Sunnyside is a comfortable community for those who want to escape the big city life. Though its residents are middle class, Dale Ewell, the father of the Ewell family, was a millionaire. He had built his fortune by running an airplane dealership.

Self-Absorbed

Besides their Sunnyside residence, the Ewells also owned a beach house on the west coast. The family had met there for a celebration but had planned to return home for Easter Sunday.

As Avitia got out of her car, she saw a neighbor standing outside the house. The neighbor told Avitia that he had received a call from Dana Ewell, Dale's 21-year-old son. Dana, who was on the west coast, was trying to reach his family, but no one was answering.

Avitia knocked on the door, but there was no answer. The security system was turned off and the door was unlocked. Avitia entered the home, then she noticed something she had never seen before: the kitchen door was closed. She walked toward the kitchen and let out a scream. She ran out of the house and called 911.

The sheriff's department arrived and entered the home; they had a triple murder on their hands.

Dana Ewell was born on January 28th, 1971. His father was the owner of Western Piper Sales Inc., where he was known to be a hard-nosed businessman who was very competitive and all about the money. The adage of 'the apple does not fall far from the tree' fit Dana well.

Like his father, Ewell was extremely competitive in everything that he did. He was also obsessed with becoming rich, and it was important to him to be admired by others.

In his freshman year at San Joaquin Memorial High School, Ewell claimed he would be a multi-millionaire by age 25. Because he was very bright, he was accepted in the honors finance program at Santa Clara University, where he wore Armani suits, silk ties, and drove a gold Mercedes Benz. His need to become rich and be admired resulted in him having few friends. Others saw him as arrogant. His obsession with being admired by others did not bother him until it backfired.

Backfire

While attending Santa Clara, he bragged that he was a financial success as a result of his trades in the stock market, his ownership of an airplane dealership, and that he was richer than his father. All of which were lies. He was still being supported by his parents. The San Jose Mercury News got word of his story and printed an article about him. Unfortunately for him, his father also read the story.

For his father, it was a slap in the face that his son would make such false claims. In his anger, he threatened to cut Dana out of his will. Upon his father's passing, Dana would inherit a portion of his father's 8-million-dollar estate. However, if his mother and sister died, he would inherit it all.

In Dana's world, money was everything. To be left out of the inheritance would be like having a death sentence imposed on him. Dana could not accept this fate. The years of resentment he had held for his father could not be concealed any longer. He had to live in his father's shadow for all these years. His father, who was living the life that Dana had to have, was now cutting him off. A burning rage took over his entire being. He would make his father pay.

The Plan

Joel Radovich was Ewell's roommate at Santa Clara. By appearance, Radovich was the polar opposite of Ewell. While Ewell dressed immaculately, Radovich had an unkempt look and dressed like a slob. While Ewell's good looks made him attractive to women, Radovich was insecure and a loner. Ewell was very goal-oriented to a fault. Radovich drifted through life.

Ewell made Radovich a deal that he could not resist. He told him of the 8-million-dollar inheritance and that he would share it with him if he murdered his family. Radovich was also money hungry and willing to do the job for him. Ewell told him to obtain a 9-mm pistol with a silencer. He also told him not to worry about the bullets; he was only to get the pistol. Radovich knew who he needed to talk to. He contacted Jack Ponce, a friend of his brother's. Ponce was experienced with guns and knew how to build silencers.

When Radovich secured the gun, Ewell met with him to plan the murder. He explained to Radovich that he and his family would be vacationing at a beach house in Pajaro Dunes, a resort near Watsonville. They would be returning the day before Easter Sunday. He also told Radovich that his father insisted on flying to the beach house, while the family would drive there.

His father had a deep fear that if the whole family traveled together, a car or a plane crash would wipe out the whole family. For this reason, Radovich should expect Ewell's mother and sister to arrive home separately from his father. He also told Radovich that he left the bullets he would need for the gun on his dad's bedroom nightstand.

For his alibi, Ewell would stay in Santa Clara and have dinner with his girlfriend Monica Zent and her parents, while his family returned home to Sunnyvale. Given that his girlfriend's father was an FBI agent, he would have the perfect person to vouch for his story. When his family left Santa Clara to return home, he would contact Radovich by pager, so that he would be prepared for their arrival home.

The Hit

On Easter Sunday of 1992, Radovich left his apartment and drove to the Ewell home in Sunny Slope. With him, he had a gun, the pager, a large plastic sheet, and a backpack. He had also shaved his entire body to avoid any chance of leaving hair at the crime scene. As he drove, he was preoccupied with only two thoughts: how he would carry out the murders and the money that awaited him.

When he arrived at the home, he walked to the front door and disabled the security system using the code that Ewell had given him. He was also able to enter the home without leaving any evidence of forced entry, as Ewell had also given him a house key. He went to Dale's room and saw the box of bullets on the nightstand. Radovich then surveyed the home to find the best location for him to station himself. The kitchen seemed like the perfect place as it was just off the hallway, and it offered a clear vantage point to fire at the family members as they walked down the hall. It also had a door, which he could close to avoid detection.

Radovich lay out the plastic tarp on the kitchen floor. He would use it to capture any evidence that he might leave. He sat on the plastic sheet with his gun loaded, and he waited. Radovich had already paged him, so he knew the family would arrive in the next few hours.

A graduate of Fresno University, Tiffany Ewell, Dana's 24-year-old sister, was the first to enter the home. She had driven home with her mother, Glee Ewell. Glee was still outside, getting the luggage out of the car. Tiffany walked through the front door, through the living room, and then proceeded down the hallway as she headed for her room. Radovich had the kitchen door slightly ajar, just enough so he could see her approaching. When she passed the door, he calmly walked out to the hallway and shot her in the back of the head. Tiffany was killed instantly, her blood emptying out on the carpeted hallway floor.

Glee, at 57 years old, was actively involved with her community and was a former public member of the State Bar Board of Governors. As she unloaded her baggage from the car, she heard a strange noise come from within the home. Concerned, she went inside to investigate.

Radovich followed the same approach with Glee as he did with Tiffany. He waited for her to pass the kitchen and shot her from behind as she passed. Before he could step out the door to shoot her, he heard her scream. He knew she had seen her daughter's body. He stepped outside the kitchen and saw her try to run. Radovich shot her, and she fell to the floor. Seeing that she was still alive, he straddled her and pointed his gun at her. Glee covered her eyes with her arms, and he shot her three more times. Her lifeless body still had her arms covering her eyes. Radovich changed the magazine in his gun and put on a new pair of rubber gloves. He only had to wait 30 minutes before Dale Ewell arrived home.

When 59-year-old Dale Ewell arrived home, he entered the home through the garage instead of using the main entrance. Doing this placed him on the other end of the hall from the kitchen. He saw the bodies of his family before him. Before he could react, he saw Radovich pointing a gun at him. He tried to run, but Radovich shot him in the back of the head. Having slaughtered the family, Radovich ransacked the house to make it look like a robbery and left the home. He drove back to his apartment and paged Dana that the job was complete.

The Investigation

Detectives arrived within minutes to the Ewell home and interviewed Avitia as the sheriff's department secured the crime scene. The bodies of the three family members were lying in pools of dried blood. Because Radovich was so well-prepared, he left no DNA evidence or shell casings behind. They also found no forced entry and concluded that the ransacking of the home was staged. The sheriff's department called Dana to inform him of his family's murder. He drove back to Sunnyside so detectives could interview him.

Dana, in his arrogance, believed he had committed the perfect crime. He had the perfect alibi. He would soon inherit his father's wealth and become a multi-millionaire. However, it was this obsession with money that would put him on the sheriff's radar. When he met with the detectives for the interview, they were taken aback by his lack of emotions for his family's deaths. At first, detectives thought he might be in shock; however, his behavior afterward made them suspicious.

When they walked him through his parent's house, they noticed he showed no reaction when he passed the spot his mother's body had been discovered. When he saw the damage to the walls where investigators dug out bullets, he demanded to know who was going to pay for the repairs.

During the joint funeral for his family, Ewell acted as though he was at a party. He seemed to be enjoying himself and showed no sign of sadness. His uncle noticed and reported his disturbing behavior to the police.

When the will was being discussed, it turned out that Ewell would not receive his father's fortune all at once. Rather, he would receive it in installments over a period of years. When Ewell heard this, he slammed his fist on the table and bellowed, "How could he do that to me?"

Ewell became a prime suspect in the murder of his family, though they had no evidence to connect him to the crime. That is, until they started looking into the financial records. Besides being the sole inheritor of his father's fortune, he also became the executor of his grandmother's trust, which contained $400,000 to provide for her needs.

A few weeks after his family's death, they discovered that out of the $800,000 he had access to, only $124,000 remained. They also found a check for $40,000 paid to his girlfriend, a check for $11,320 paid to Radovich for flying lessons, and a check for $200,000 paid to his own attorney.

Detectives tracked down Radovich and interviewed him. Radovich informed Ewell that he was visited by the detectives. From that point on, Ewell and Radovich avoided the detectives and would not return their calls. They did not respond to their requests for follow-up interviews.

Ewell was relaxing in his apartment one weekend when there was a knock on the door. When he answered the door, it was the detectives. They asked him if they could come in to talk. With a smug look on his face, Ewell started to close the door on the detectives when one of them announced to him, "We believe Radovich killed your parents."

Detectives watched as Ewell turned white as a sheet. Ewell insisted that he did not know anyone by that name. Though they did not know at the time that Radovich had done the killings, Ewell's reaction told them they were on the right track.

Detectives then revisited Radovich, who, unlike Ewell, could not hold up to their pressure. While he did not confess to the killings, he allowed them to search his apartment. Detectives discovered the pager and a few other items of interest. Radovich permitted them to take the items to examine.

With a judge's permission, detectives were able to make a replica of Radovich's pager. This allowed them to intercept any messages between the two. They returned the pager to Radovich and continued their investigation by placing him under surveillance.

While they had no evidence to support their theory, they believed Ewell was involved because he was the one who stood to benefit from the murders of his family. The conversations they monitored between Radovich and Ewell confirmed to them that Ewell was guilty; however, it still was not enough. What broke their case was when they learned about Ponce.

Ponce confessed to the detectives that he had obtained the gun for Radovich but denied any knowledge of the murders. He stated Radovich wanted the gun to sell for a profit. Ponce was offered immunity for his testimony against Ewell and Radovich, which he took.

Sentencing

Because of the complexity of the case, detectives constructed a timeline of the information from their investigation that stretched 100 feet, which led to Ewell and Radovich being arrested in March of 1995. They went on trial on December 16th, 1997, which lasted for four months.

During the trial, over 100 witnesses were called.

Both Ewell and Radovich received life sentences without any chance of parole.

Ewell is serving his sentence at the Protective Housing Unit of California State Prison located in Corcoran.

Conclusion

SPREE KILLERS ARE A SUB-GROUP OF KILLERS known as rampage killers, which also includes mass murderers. The characteristics of spree killers are that feel they have been rejected by society and that the world is out to get them. They lose their connection with the human family and feel like they are a failure in life, that their life is no longer worth living.

Many of them develop a love for guns and for the power that they feel it gives them. They embark on a killing spree to end their own incessant suffering, while at the same time fatally lashing out at those who they feel victimized by.

It is for this reason that most spree killers kill themselves when they have accomplished their goal.

The reason why spree killers are usually men is that our traditional societal norms tell us that a real man stands up for themselves. Taking a final stand lets them show the world that they are powerful.

All the spree killers profiled in this book share a common element; they never felt accepted in their world. They all experienced indicators of past traumatic events that were never addressed. These indicators, along with their sense of hopelessness, led all the individuals profiled in this book to become spree killers.

Priscilla Ford, Jared Lee Loughner, and Jennifer San Marco had mental illnesses that never received proper treatment.

Adam Lanza and Christopher Harper-Mercer were suspected of having Asperger's Syndrome, which is no longer considered a mental illness. Their conditions also never received proper attention. Brenda Spencer and Charles Joseph Whitman both had physical damage to their brains.

The rest of the individuals profiled in this book surely had experienced things in their lives, that when combined with a sense of isolation and helplessness, led them to do the unspeakable.

None of the individuals in this book were born this way. As long as people feel marginalized by society, some of them will strike back with a vengeance.

This marks the end of all the stories. On the next page, you will find a preview to other cola-hearted killers...

Continue Your Exploration Into

The Murderous Minds

Excerpt From Murderous Minds Volume 1

I
Michael David Clagett

MICHAEL D. CLAGETT SAW THE PRISON GUARDS approaching his cell. It was time.

One guard unlocked the cell door, and two other guards secured him in handcuffs and leg shackles. Clagett exchanged a few words with them as they started walking in silence toward the room of the corrections center where his execution would take place.

For Clagett, the brief walk down the cold, sterile hallways of the Greensville Correction Center seemed to take forever. It was not because he dreaded what awaited him. On the contrary, Clagett welcomed his execution.

He was offered two options for his execution; lethal injection or the electric chair. He chose the electric chair. He thought it was ironic. He felt he deserved to die; yet, around twenty people had gathered outside the prison to hold a candlelight vigil. The gathering was organized by Virginians for Alternatives to the Death Penalty. They sang songs and read passages from the Bible.

The thirty-nine-year-old Clagett would be the second inmate executed by electric chair since the state of Virginia passed a law offering inmates a choice. He had been on death row for six years and was serving five death sentences, one for each person he had killed on June 30, 1994.

His trial ended with the jury convicting him of four counts of capital murder in the commission of a robbery, along with one count of multiple homicide murder.

As the guards led him into the room where his execution would take place, he saw a small group of people, some family members of his victims, seated in the viewing room. They would witness his execution. Some were standing. Two of those standing were his mother and his wife Karen, who he had married while on death row. Both were in tears. Though he fully accepted his fate, he would die with unanswered questions; why did he do it? Why did he allow his girlfriend, Denise, talk him into killing those people?

Power Play

Denise Holsinger separated from her husband, Randell Holsinger, in 1993, and met Clagett soon after. Clagett was everything her husband was not. While her husband was a first-class petty officer in the Navy, Clagett was chronically unemployed, had a history of committing domestic violence, and a long history of drinking and using drugs. She had her own demons and engaged in drinking and drug use. She had three children, whom she left with her husband as she did not feel she could deal with the responsibility. She just wanted out, and Clagett appealed to her because of his wild streak. She'd grown tired of being the proper Navy wife. Clagett's irresponsible manner provided the freedom to express her discontent with life.

Holsinger met Clagett at her place of work, the Witchduck Inn. Located on Pembroke Boulevard, in Virginia Beach, Witchduck Inn is a tavern and restaurant, and Clagett was a regular there. Clagett frequented the tavern so often that he considered the bar owner, Lam Van Son, a friend. Son had fled his native South

Vietnam during the communist takeover. He had fought with U.S. soldiers, as he was part of South Vietnam's Special Forces unit.

When South Vietnam fell to the communist in 1975, Son was placed in a re-education camp. Son escaped the camp and traveled to Thailand by boat before coming to America. He had settled in Lynchburg, where he married Lanna Le Son in 1988.

Holsinger rented a small apartment, and Clagett moved in with her. He spent most of the time lying around the house getting stoned. Holsinger would join him when she arrived home from work. While Clagett did not contribute to the household, Holsinger allowed it.

It put her in a position where she felt she held power in the relationship, and that power came without resistance. In her marriage, she felt she had to play the role of the dutiful wife; it was different with Clagett. In their relationship, she was the one with the job and the money, and she was the one who offered him female attention.

Terminated

It was in June of 1994, the demons within Holsinger and Clagett collided to create an explosion of violence that sent the community into shock. Holsinger had been pocketing money from her job at the Witchduck Inn. She had been doing it for months; to help support the drug habit that had begun to consume both her and Clagett.

Unfortunately for Holsinger, her stealing caught up with her. Her boss, Lam Van Son, caught on to what she was doing and fired her June 28. Holsinger was livid when Son told her that he was letting her go. Instead of being grateful that Son was not going to report her crime to the police, Holsinger cursed him and blamed him for being paranoid about the whole thing. She insisted she was innocent.

Giving in

Holsinger arrived home after work to find Clagett in the living room, inhaling from a bong. He also had a bottle of whiskey. Holsinger grabbed the bong and took a few puffs before drinking from the bottle. She told Clagett about being fired as the drugs and alcohol took effect. Clagett reached out to comfort her but she pushed him away. She was determined she was going to make Son pay.

Clagett got up from the couch and took her in his arms, telling her it would be all right; somehow, they would make it. Clagett's attempts to console her were not working; he could see that she remained upset. He thought he knew what would help. He ran his drunk, stoned hands all over her before pulling her into the bedroom. They had wild and intense sex; the kind he knew would get her to release the pressure she kept inside.

The next morning, as the two of them lay in bed, Holsinger divulged her plan. She wanted Clagett with her when she robbed the Witchduck. She stroked his chest and told him after they got the money, they could get away and find a new place to live.

She had ideas of going to Mexico or Canada. Clagett seemed hesitant in agreeing to her plan. The worst offense he was ever jailed for was committing domestic violence against his last two wives. Because of the brutality of his crimes, he had been jailed for several years. Still, he wanted to please Holsinger. She convinced him by comparing them to Bonnie and Clyde. They would be free and famous.

He wanted Holsinger's approval. It led him to agree. In his mind, Clagett had nothing to lose and everything to gain. For the next two days, the couple would binge on drugs and alcohol.

The Witchduck Assault

On June 30, thirty-one-year-old Karen Rounds arrived for her shift at the Witchduck Inn. She had been hired by Son to replace Holsinger as their new waitress. A Pennsylvania native, Rounds moved to Virginia Beach with her husband, Kevin Rounds.

Rounds had been a nurse but looking for a career change. She had worked as a nurse at a state prison while her husband was in the Navy. When they moved to Virginia Beach, she got a job working at the Maryview Medical Center; a clinic located in Churchland. She quit her job to go back to school to study computers.

Her new job at the Witchduck Inn would provide her with some spending money while attending classes. Both Karen and her husband knew Clagett as they often saw him when they went to Witchduck. Karen found Clagett to be creepy, but her husband had reassured her that he would not harm anyone.

When she entered the Witchduck Inn, she was greeted by Abdelaziz Gren, one of the regulars. Gren was born in Morocco and came to the United States so he could live the American Dream, which included owning his own business and having his own home and car. He had learned English and attended college while living in Morocco so that he would be prepared when he arrived in the 'promised land.' He spoke fluent Arabic, English, and French. Upon arriving in America, Gren attended Old Dominion University, while working in his family's restaurant.

Everyone who knew him spoke of his big heart and how he would help anybody in need. During Thanksgiving, Gren had been taking a walk along the Lynnhaven River, where he came across a fisherman. The fisherman was taking fish below the size limit. Gren brought this to the attention of the man, who replied that he depended on his catch to feed his family.

Gren went to a local grocery store and bought food for the man and his family. He once told his sister that his altruism came from his gratitude for all the opportunities he had received since coming to this country. Gren frequently gave Clagett money so he could buy food, and would occasionally treat him to drinks at the Witchduck.

Rounds entered the kitchen where she saw Son talking to Wendel Parrish. Parrish was the tavern's cook and handyman. He was born in Prince George, Virginia, and later moved to Hampton Roads. He attended Bayside High School, where he graduated in

1981. The thirty-two-year-old Parrish would often treat Clagett to meals at the tavern.

Rounds was busy that day as the Witchduck attracted a larger crowd than normal as Son had the World Cup on the tavern's big-screen television. Later that night, the crowd emptied into the street. There were only a few patrons left, one of which was Gren. Rounds walked through the rear exit of the tavern and into the humid night air to take a break. What she did not realize was that it would be the last work break she would ever take.

When Rounds finished her break, she stepped back inside and returned to the kitchen. She saw Son and Parrish working. Right off the kitchen was a small room where Son's five-year-old son, Joshua, was sleeping. Son frequently brought Joshua to work as his wife worked.

She went back to the dining area to check on her customers when she spotted Clagett and Holsinger. Holsinger was playing pool while Clagett was at a nearby table.

Seeing Holsinger and Clagett made her uncomfortable. She had a bad feeling about Clagett. Now that Holsinger had been fired, she did not trust her, either. Little did Rounds know, she was minutes away from Virginia Beach's first quadruple murder.

As per Holsinger's plan, Clagett monitored the activity in the small tavern as Holsinger played pool. Holsinger looked at Clagett, waiting for him to make eye contact with her; their mutual eye contact was the signal to make their move. The audience for the World Cup had left along with most of the regulars. The remaining people in the tavern were Son, Parrish, Rounds, and Gren.

Holsinger gave Clagett a nod and rushed to the counter, jumping over it. She went straight for the cash register as Clagett pulled out a .357-Magnum revolver and joined her behind the counter. He ordered everyone in the restaurant to gather in the kitchen and get on the floor.

Everyone but Parrish complied. He refused to give in to the threats and remained on his barstool. Holsinger tried to get Clagett to 'do it!' Clagett hesitated. Holsinger was insistent that he comply. She repeated her order. Clagett collected his nerve, placed the barrel of his gun inches from Parrish's face and pulled the trigger.

The bullet passed through Parrish's head, and he slumped forward on the bar. Rounds screamed in terror as she lay on the floor. Son and Gren remained silent and did not move. Holsinger ordered Clagett to continue shooting the rest of them. One by one, Clagett shot each person on the floor execution-style, placing his gun to the back of their head and shooting. When he was done, the kitchen floor was covered in blood.

Holsinger grabbed four hundred dollars from the register. A small pittance for their efforts. When they were about to take off, Holsinger noticed Son's son, Joshua, sleeping in the other room. Holsinger ordered Clagett to shoot the child. Telling him they could not leave any witnesses.

Clagett could not pull the trigger on the sleeping child. Fearful of waiting for a second longer, Holsinger fled without Clagett. She drove off in their car, leaving Clagett behind. Still strung out from the drugs and alcohol from the previous two days, Clagett felt a deep sense of fear as he stared at the bloody, dead bodies. He screamed and ran out of the tavern into the dark, humid night.

At midnight, one of the regulars, Richard T. Reed, arrived at the Witchduck Inn for a drink. The Witchduck was open until two in the morning; however, Reed found the front door locked. He heard music playing inside, so he went around to the back entrance. To his surprise, the rear entrance was unlocked. Normally, the back door was locked.

Upon entering the tavern, he was met with a very bloody scene: bloodied bodies on the kitchen floor and Parrish slumped over the bar.

He called 911 and was soon joined by another regular, who was well-liked by Joshua. Joshua called the man "Uncle Richie." Knowing Joshua frequently slept at the restaurant, he ran inside.

With a singular focus, the man made his way past the dead bodies, over the blood-covered floor, and reached the room. To his relief, Joshua was unharmed but terrified. The man comforted Joshua and carried him out of the restaurant, making sure to cover his eyes.

Minutes later, Joshua was sitting in the back seat of a squad car with "Uncle Richie," who was comforting him. Both of them watched as bodies, covered by blankets, were pushed by on gurneys as first responders loaded them into the back of the waiting ambulances.

Apprehended

On July 1, 1994, Virginia Beach Police Officer Donna Malcolm was on patrol when she received a call requesting an officer respond to a disturbance. When she arrived at the address, the resident told Malcolm that a man was sleeping in the bushes of her front yard.

Malcolm arrested the man for public intoxication and brought him to police headquarters, where he was questioned by Detective Yoakum. The man Yoakum was interviewing was Clagett.

What Clagett did not know was that police had arrested Holsinger earlier. She had been pulled over for reckless driving when she had fled the crime scene. Because Holsinger provided a description of Clagett, Yoakum had a strong suspicion that the man he was talking to was the murderer; however, Clagett continued to deny any involvement with the Witchduck Inn killings.

Yoakum deceived Clagett, by telling him he had been caught by the tavern's security cameras at the time of the murders. Hearing this, Clagett stopped denying his involvement and confessed to the killings.

The police detective told Clagett that was exactly what they would be asking the court. His rant during confession: 'Fry me; I'm not gonna live. I don't want the taxpayers supporting me. I did it. Yeah, I did it. I did it all. All-by-my-fucking-self. Let that little cunt go free. I did it all. I did it all buddy. And the worst thing was Lam (Son) was my buddy!'

Later that same day, a reporter from WTKR Channel 3 news asked Clagett if he was guilty of the charges. Clagett replied to the reporter, 'Yes. I shot every one of them.'

Clagett later reversed himself by claiming that his confessions of guilt were made while he was still under the influence of drugs. He was put on trial. The ten-day trial ended with the jury finding Clagett guilty of four counts of capital murder, one count of multiple homicide capital murder, robbery, and the use of a firearm.

On October 24, 1995, Clagett was placed on death row.

A year later, Clagett married his first cousin, Karen Elaine Sparks, in a jailhouse ceremony.

On July 6, 2000, Clagett was strapped to the electric chair while some family members of the victims, Clagett's mother, and his new wife, looked on in silence. Clagett was expressionless at first, then broke down while he apologized to the victim's families.

Once he was secured in the chair, the first of two electrical charges were discharged. The first charge was eighteen hundred twenty-five volts and lasted thirty seconds, while the second charge was two hundred and forty volts for sixty seconds. He was pronounced dead after the second shock.

He would be the last person in the United States to be executed using the electric chair.

Holsinger is serving five life sentences plus twenty-three years in the Fluvanna Correctional Center for Women.

The End of **The Preview**

Visit us at **truecrimeseven.com** or scan QR Code using your phone's **camera app** to find more true crime books and other cool goodies.

About True Crime Seven

True Crime Seven is about exploring the stories of the sinful minds in this world. From unknown murderers to well-known serial killers. It is our goal to create a place for true crime enthusiasts to satisfy their morbid curiosities while sparking new ones.

Our writers come from all walks of life but with one thing in common, and that is they are all true crime enthusiasts. You can learn more about them below:

Ryan Becker is a True Crime author who started his writing journey in late 2016. Like most of you, he loves to explore the process of how individuals turn their darkest fantasies into a reality. Ryan has always had a passion for storytelling. So, writing is the best output for him to combine his fascination with psychology and true crime. It is Ryan's goal for his readers to experience the full immersion with the dark reality of the world, just like how he used to in his younger days.

Nancy Alyssa Veysey is a writer and author of true crime books, including the bestselling, Mary Flora Bell: The Horrific True Story Behind an Innocent Girl Serial Killer. Her medical degree and work in the field of forensic psychology, along with postgraduate studies in criminal justice, criminology, and pre-law, allow her to bring a unique perspective to her writing.

Kurtis-Giles Veysey is a young writer who began his writing career in the fantasy genre. In late 2018, he parlayed his love and knowledge of history into writing nonfiction accounts of true crime stories that occurred in centuries past. Told from a historical perspective, Kurtis-Giles brings these victims and their killers back to life with vivid descriptions of these heinous crimes.

Kelly Gaines is a writer from Philadelphia. Her passion for storytelling began in childhood and carried into her college career. She received a B.A. in English from Saint Joseph's University in 2016, with a concentration in Writing Studies. Now part of the real world, Kelly enjoys comic books, history documentaries, and a good scary story. In her true-crime work, Kelly focuses on the motivations of the killers and backgrounds of the victims to draw a complete picture of each individual. She deeply enjoys writing for True Crime Seven and looks forward to bringing more spine-tingling tales to readers.

James Parker, the pen-name of a young writer from New Jersey, who started his writing journey with play-writing. He has always been fascinated with the psychology of murderers and how the media might play a role in their creation. James loves to constantly test out new styles and ideas in his writing so one day he can find something cool and unique to himself.

Brenda Brown is a writer and an illustrator-cartoonist. Her art can be found in books distributed both nationally and internationally. She has also written many books related to her graduate degree in psychology and her minor in history. Like many true crime enthusiasts, she loves exploring the minds of those who see the world as a playground for expressing the darker side of themselves—the side that people usually locked up and hid from scrutiny.

Genoveva Ortiz is a Los Angeles-based writer who began her career writing scary stories while still in college. After receiving a B.A. in English in 2018, she shifted her focus to nonfiction and the real-life horrors of crime and unsolved mysteries. Together with True Crime Seven, she is excited to further explore the world of true crime through a social justice perspective.

You can learn more about us and our writers at:

https://truecrimeseven.com/about/

For updates about new releases, as well as exclusive promotions, join True Crime Seven readers' group and you can also **receive a free book today.** Thank you and see you soon.
Sign up at: **freebook.truecrimeseven.com/**

Or **scan QR Code using your phone's camera app.**

Dark Fantasies Turned Reality

Prepare yourself, we're not going to **hold back on details or cut out any of the gruesome truths...**

Made in the USA
Monee, IL
05 November 2023